# The Cultural Advantage

# The Cultural Advantage

## A New Model
## for Succeeding
## with Global Teams

## Mijnd Huijser

INTERCULTURAL PRESS
A Nicholas Brealey Publishing Company

BOSTON • LONDON

First published by Intercultural Press, a Nicholas Brealey
Publishing Company, in 2006.

Intercultural Press, a division
of Nicholas Brealey Publishing
100 City Hall Plaza, Suite 501
Boston, MA 02108 USA
Tel: +617-523-3801
Fax: +617-523-3708
www.interculturalpress.com

Nicholas Brealey Publishing
3-5 Spafield Street, Clerkenwell
London, EC1R 4QB, UK
Tel: +44-(0)-207-239-0360
Fax: +44-(0)-207-239-0370
www.nicholasbrealey.com

Also published by Dutch Publication: Business Contact Amsterdam 2005

Printed in the UK by Good News Press

10   09   08   07   06                                         1   2   3   4   5

ISBN: 978-1-931930-28-4

**Library of Congress Cataloging-in-Publication Data**

Huijser, Mijnd.
   The cultural advantage : a new model for succeeding with global teams /
Mijnd Huijser.
      p. cm.
   Includes bibliographical references.
   ISBN-13: 978-1-931930-28-4
   ISBN-10: 1-931930-28-7
   1. Diversity in the workplace—Management.   2. International business
enterprises—Employees.   3. International business enterprises—Personnel
management.   4. Teams in the workplaces—Management.   5. Multiculturalism.
I. Title.
HF5549.5.M5H85   2006
658.3008—dc22                                         2006001808

# Praise for the Dutch Edition of
## *The Cultural Advantage*

"Very accessible and inspiring, with appealing examples for everyone preferring cultural intelligence to conflict management."

Floris Oskam, Unilever Europe, Director, Supply Management

"Culture tends to cause a disorderly jumble and little understanding. This book puts an end to all that confusion."

Paul Meerts, Clingendael Institute of International Relations, Deputy Director, Training & Education

"I recommend this work to everybody who rises to the challenges of cultural integration and cooperation in alliances or joint ventures."

Rob Woldberg, Nissan Europe, General Manager

"Communication is key in the twenty-first century. Understanding is a prerequisite to success. The model presented in this book is concise and practical, contributing to the reader's cross-cultural management skills."

Hennie Stegen, DSM International, Program Manager, International Human Resources

"This book helped me grasp the challenges we encounter in our global project teams, where East meets West."

Hans Brouwhuis, Philips Semiconductors Japan, Senior Director & Telecom Product Creation

# A Testimonial

To: Mijnd Huijser mijnd@cmc-net.org
Subject: *The Cultural Advantage*
From: Henk.Thijssen
Date: Wed, 26 Jan 2005 07:16:08 +0800

Dear Mijnd,

I hope that my review reaches you in time. I was quite busy and, to be honest, your manuscript got somewhat lost in my briefcase. However, when I finally got to it, during a long flight from Shanghai to Amsterdam, I read it in one go. I am not a reading type of person; normally it takes me ages to finish a book. But not this time. I am deeply impressed by its readability. Especially your presentation of everyday situations to illustrate complex cultural issues makes the book fascinating.

This is my succinct feedback:
The book offers insights in complex cultural differences using recognizable examples. It reads like a novel. Your model, the Model of Freedom, is presented dashingly, and enhances reciprocal understanding and respect between cultures cooperating in an organization.

The Model of Freedom, applied in our company, has already resulted in improved cooperation between the Chinese and the Dutch.

To me it seems that the book is very valuable for all European-Asian cooperation, not in the least because of the plainness of the model you introduce. At last, a book that goes beyond the common explanations of "loss of face."

> Kind regards,
> Henk Thijssen
> Director Industrial Technology Center Philips Semiconductors
> China Technology Center
> Philips Mobile Display Systems Shanghai
> China

# Acknowledgments

I am heavily indebted to the companies and institutions that called me in for assignments; I could not have written this book without them. Their trust in me has generated a mutual learning process. My special thanks go to:

*Accenture* Bratislava, Prague, Paris, London, Lisbon, Milan, Nice; *Unilever* Brussels, Hamburg, Geneva, Bangkok, New York; *Philips* Heerlen, Zurich, Shanghai, Hong Kong, Kobe; *Nissan-Renault* Amsterdam, Paris, Barcelona, *Statskonsult* Oslo; *IBM* Copenhagen; *KPN Mobile* The Hague; *Telephonica* Madrid; *Rabobank International* Utrecht; *DZ-Bank* Frankfurt; *Mitsubishi Motors* Amsterdam; *PricewaterhouseCoopers* Amsterdam; *Clifford Chance* Frankfurt; *Canon Europe* Amsterdam, London; *3M-Germany* Neuss, Munich; *Johnson & Johnson* Los Angeles, Brussels; *ING-bank* Amsterdam; *DSM* Geleen; *Clingendael Institute of International Relations* The Hague; *University of Amsterdam*; *University of Frankfurt*; *VU Academic Hospital Amsterdam*; *The European Institute of Purchasing Management* Geneva; *Swedish School of Management* Stockholm; and the *British Council* London.

# Contents

# Introduction

W hile working in Africa as an International Red Cross official, my Swiss colleague Ariane once met a Touareg who said to her, "You have blue eyes." She felt flattered, as she had at other occasions when people complimented her on her bright blue eyes. Later she discovered that the Touareg was expressing alarm. Dealing with blue-eyed camels is the worst that can happen to a Touareg. Those beasts are unmanageable!

We tend to interpret and give meaning to words and behaviors by referring to our own experiences and social environment. But without mutual cultural understanding, professionals who regularly interact with cultures other than their own are plagued by miscommunication and worse. This book will help you become aware of your framework for giving meaning and your own cultural biases, and it offers a tool to help you find out more about the frameworks and biases of other cultures.

## The Advantage of Cultural Differences

When pondering upon a title for this book, ideas like *Champions in the International Arena*, *An American in Europe*, or *The Profit of*

*Culture* crossed my mind. I was searching for a banner that would express how the model I present here empowers professionals in a globalizing world to take full advantage of the cultural differences they encounter. Because that is exactly what this book aims to do: trigger and sharpen your cultural intelligence in order to increase your effectiveness when working in global teams. Cultural intelligence helps us achieve better results on a national, organizational, vocational, and even on a project team level. Hence the final title, *The Cultural Advantage*, which neatly conveys the promise behind the book's content.

What makes this book different from other, often excellent, books on intercultural cooperation is that the Model of Freedom, which is the basis for this book, is rooted in the real-world experiences of professionals in international companies. For over twelve years I have created, tested, and adjusted this model through my work as an international consultant, training intercultural teams at Fortune 500 companies. The model gradually developed into a solid tool, visualizing differences between cultures, and delivering an "all-season ticket" to different organizational and national cultures.

## Who Should Read This Book?

Beware: this book is not about How to do Business in China, Holland, Spain . . . or any other country. Nor will you find lists of do's and don'ts. I am not offering you a fish for today's meal, but a rod to catch fish for the rest of your international career.

*The Cultural Advantage* is for executives, managers, and other professionals who work in international project and task teams, or who on a daily basis deal in some way or another with colleagues from different cultures. It is for people whose international working environment challenges them to cope with a wide variety of communication styles and convictions about what is right, just, or timely.

For practical reasons, the examples in this book have a limited scope. I focus on Americans working outside the United States, Britons working on the Continent, and Europeans cooperating with other Europeans. Because China and Japan have become important players in the international business world, I also pay special attention to the cultural characteristics of these countries, so this book might well serve Chinese and Japanese readers who want to understand more of the Western management styles. As Takeo Fujisawa, one of the founders of Honda Corporations, once stated: "Eastern and Western management styles are 95 percent the same, but differ in every important aspect."

I am aware that professionals work cross-culturally with many important nations whose cultural characteristics I do not discuss extensively. But over the years my experience has been that Zambians, Turks, Arabs, Brazilians, Indians, and Malaysians, to mention just a few, easily recognize their culture in the Model of Freedom and find it easy to adapt it to suit their purposes.

## Background on the Model of Freedom

Anyone seeking research, theories, and models to sharpen their cultural intelligence is inevitably directed to two Dutch gurus[1]; Geert Hofstede and Fons Trompenaars. Both have founded their own schools of thought,[2] and these schools seem hard to reconcile.

---

[1]"Guru" means "teacher" in Hindi. I use the word here in its original meaning.
[2]Appendix 1 contains a short summary of Trompenaars' and Hofstede's theories.

According to Hofstede, culture does not change or ultimately changes so slowly that his data, assembled at the end of the sixties and the beginning of the seventies, are still valid in the twenty-first century. Trompenaars, on the other hand, defines culture as a process of changes, and our ability to adapt to them. He performs continuous research to refresh his data.

Since 1993, I have worked for about three years with the Hofstede-associated Institute for Training in Intercultural Management (ITIM), and for about the same length of time with Fons Trompenaars' organization, Trompenaars-Hampden-Turner Culture for Business (THT). Thus, I have had the chance to learn first-hand all the subtleties of the models and training methods of both gurus. More importantly, during my assignments I could watch my clients respond to both Trompenaars' and Hofstede's concepts, which provided me with valuable insights into each theory's wealth and limitations. The limitations partly originate from the fact that both researchers use questionnaires to collect their data. Yet no matter how ingenious questionnaires can be, people remain unpredictable in their interpretations of questions, and the validity of their answers becomes biased. That may explain, for example, why the French score high on "individualism" in Hofstede's model and low in Trompenaars' model. People interpret questions differently if they are differently formulated. This may lead to surprising research outcomes because of a different and unpredicted understanding of the meaning.

In the work of researchers like Edgar Schein, Robert Quinn, David Kolb, and Timothy Leary, I found concepts that served as the basic components of the Model of Freedom (MoF).[3] I refined these components, using my clients' responses to the data of Hofstede and Trompenaars. To solve the problem of distorted questionnaire answers, and therefore inadequate scores, I applied the Appreciative In-

---

[3]See Appendix 2 for a more detailed description of the origin of my Model.

quiry method.[4] This means that instead of working with question-naires, I talked with professionals directly, asking them to emphasize the positive aspects of what they perceived to be complex intercultural situations. I'd simply ask: Where were you successful? In such discussions the issue is not merely personal intentions, but verifiable implementation: what did I do to bring about this success? In my experience, the Appreciative Inquiry method is an excellent way to prevent people from hiding behind politically correct answers, and from over- or underestimating themselves. With the feedback of some 5,000 internationally operating managers, gathered through this method, I could adjust the scores of both gurus.

The MoF contains four dimensions in which all national and organizational cultures can be categorized. The value of the model lies not in the categorization itself, but in how it allows us to visualize the differences between cultures. Not the precise scores of individual managers are of interest, not even the precise scores of organizations or nations, but the determination of their cultural orientations as opposed to those of others. This has proven to be an enormously advantageous learning method.

## Structure of the Book

Chapter 1 launches the book with a hypothetical case study, which introduces us to an interesting group working for an international organization. We learn about their various expectations, aspirations, and ambitions as they prepare to realize a common goal. As we will see, the differences in their cultural orientation will make this quite a challenge.

---

[4]Charles Elliott, *Locating the Energy for Change: An Introduction to Appreciative Inquiry*, IISD, Winnipeg, Canada, 1999.

In Chapter 2, I describe elements of culture that are universal and will be recognized by people from all over the world. Despite the huge variety in cultures, common values definitely exist. We are not from different planets.

In Chapter 3, I assemble the Model of Freedom and present its components and characteristics.

Chapter 4 explains the four cultural orientations — four different perceptions of reality — that are represented in the Model of Freedom.

The following chapters discuss topics that require a high level of cultural intelligence. I will show you how to achieve this level.

A critical topic is leadership, covered in Chapter 5. The achievements of an organization highly depend on its leadership, especially since leaders nowadays are expected to be future-oriented and capable of managing complex operations. We'll discuss what makes a good leader in an intercultural setting.

Next, in Chapter 6, we'll discuss how communication in intercultural teams can easily degenerate because of misunderstandings and friction among members of the group. I will show you how you can use the MoF to deal more effectively with a range of culturally biased styles of communication.

Chapter 7 is about meetings and decision-making processes. The gathering of various cultures can easily turn a conference room into a battlefield. I will clarify the preferred styles of certain cultures and indicate how meetings can be conducted more effectively by recognizing and anticipating these styles.

Chapter 8 explores how to manage a change process in an intercultural context. For some cultures, change is a source of inspiration; for others, it is a threat. Without using cultural intelligence, you will spend most of your valuable time managing conflicts instead of moving your team or project forward.

Chapter 9 deals with corporate cultures. Each organization has its own corporate culture, and within the organization branches and departments have their own subcultures. Furthermore, every phase in the life cycle of an organization has its own typical culture. The MoF offers managers and other professionals the tools to convert the tensions in a corporate culture into a source of energy.

In conclusion, all cultural knowledge acquired in the previous chapters will be integrated in Chapter 10, and we'll take a look at how a winning intercultural team functions.

For readers who may be interested in the concepts of Hofstede and Trompenaars, I present their ideas in boxes. Those readers who do not wish to be distracted by additional scientific theory may skip these boxes.

Our cultural preferences obviously do not only manifest themselves in our work; often they are even more clearly visible in other social and artistic means of expression. Take the way people in different cultures enjoy their meals, or the way in which advertisers present their products in commercials. Throughout the book are boxes with "Cultural Highlights," which examine these kinds of expressions and their significance in a particular culture. These cultural highlights can help you have a better understanding of national cultures and their influence on management styles.

# 1

# From Hurricane to Drizzle

"Hi, Darling. Please, can I call you back in a minute?" Rick just can't deal with his wife's problems right now. He just had a terrible day, and the Amsterdam expressway is jam-packed. Oh Lord, he realizes, she probably wanted to remind him to pick up Jake from basketball practice. He had completely forgotten about his son. Anyway, first priority now is to keep an eye on the road. These Dutch keep switching lanes. Please, don't let me ruin my job, my fatherhood, and my car all in one day.

Rick is preoccupied with the team meeting that took all day. It had been the kick-off of his ambitious project, and the reason to move with his family from Chicago to Amsterdam. He had anxiously anticipated this day. "Cheer up, old chap," his boss at Em-Log Worldwide had said, jokingly, when he was about to leave for Europe. He knew that it would be tough to get all these stubborn egos from the old world heading in the same direction. But Rick Delano was the best man for the job, the head office told him. And to be honest, Rick could not disagree.

His mission was clear: all European EmLog branches should start using the same new software for all logistic systems. The timetable was clear as well: the systems should be operational within one year. And his team was extremely talented: IT people from Germany, France, the United Kingdom, the Netherlands, Italy, Spain, and Sweden, and a guy from Japan who would investigate if the software would also be applicable in Japan, China, and South Korea. All of them engineers, the kind of people he could easily get along with.

He had been in great shape for the kick-off meeting. After six miles of jogging and three cups of decaf, his passionate, zealous welcome speech went over easily. He offered a vibrant PowerPoint presentation, pressing for clear objectives and milestones. He was confident that this meeting would turn out to be prolific.

But now he feels dejected. If pressed, he would euphemistically characterize the team's mood as indifferent. *Obstructive* and *hair-splitting*, however, are terms that come a lot closer to what he feels he encountered with the team. He just can't believe how this meeting, launched like a hurricane, could die down in such a drizzle.


And now for a glass of really good wine. Jean-Jacques hums on his way to his hotel. The three of them, Giulio, Carlos, and he, had washed away that tiresome meeting in a typical Dutch café on the Rembrandt Square with beer and peanuts. He always enjoyed these rare occasions to hang out with his Italian and Spanish colleagues. Naturally, Giulio had treated himself to another new car, which he caressed with words like a lover. And Carlos performed a hilarious imitation of the German, Günther, telling his deadly boring story chock-full of legalese. He also did a perfect imitation of the American team leader: "Guys!!! You're the best team I've ever seen!!!"

Whatever. All that pep talk. What's it got to do with me, Jean-Jacques wonders, walking along the Amsterdam canals. EmLog's head office in Chicago had selected France as the first country to implement the new software. So this afternoon, Jean-Jacques did a presentation on the technical adjustments judged necessary by the Paris office. True, he might have been a bit tedious, not unlike Günther, but he felt it was vital to explain his point of view on such a sweeping operation, and to elaborate on its significance, not only for their own company, but for the future of the car industry as such. He would have liked to dwell a bit longer on that branch. Car manufacturers were their most important clients, and very interesting developments were going on. But he had restrained himself, just like he had succeeded in restraining the American, who was pressing for speed Rick had immediately started to push "his" team into a rigid timetable. Yeah, right, tricky Ricky. First thing Jean-Jacques would do upon arriving at his hotel was make a phone call to Paris.

"Unbelievable, that Englishman. Such nerve! Just walked out during my presentation to make a phone call. I heard him comment to the Swede, 'I can't swallow all those numbers, I'll read them later.'" Günther is on his cell with Dieter, his assistant, after having installed himself in the Schiphol business lounge. He had to get this insulting experience off his chest.

EmLog head office had asked Frankfurt to adapt American demands to European laws and standards. So Günther not only called in Dieter, but also an entire team of lawyers. Ten, twelve hours of research a day were not unusual, and they had made a real effort to prepare a well-ordered presentation. Tough work, but he had felt comfortable with the assignment. Their research would spare the other European branches a tremendous amount of time.

Günther wipes some cappuccino froth from his moustache, and continues to air his indignation. "And Rick Delano, you'd expect him to have read our report before the meeting. Well, I'm sure he didn't. He kept glancing through his pile of papers with this annoying smile on his face. And after my presentation he immediately passed on to the next subject. In my opinion, those Americans don't want to be bothered by the legal implications of their plans. They want everything smooth and fast. I should think we've clearly demonstrated that there is no such thing."

"Tell me," asks Dieter on the phone, "has anything been decided? Any more work in it for me tonight? I actually wanted to take my girlfriend to the movies."

"Decided? Nothing, of course," Günther replies, at last a bit pleased. "Jean-Jacques and I took care of that."


Jan-Hein is comfortably seated on the couch with his cat Minou snoring on his lap. The team meeting today took a long time, but turned out better than expected.

Beforehand, Annette, his boss, had warned him not to be too candid about his unfortunate adventure in Belgium, but he hadn't cared. Look, it wasn't *his* fault that his IT knowledge hadn't fired over there. Besides, the team had profited a lot from his interventions. They had better know from the start which obstacles he had encountered in Antwerp. Everyone could benefit from that, especially that self-confident team leader, Rick. If that man could have his way, he would map out the whole project for the coming year.

Which is nonsense, of course. With some effort, Jan-Hein had succeeded in catching Rick's attention with his plea to introduce flexibility in the planning. Things should be readjusted gradually, depending on their progress. He assumes that Rick got the message.

Jan-Hein thinks there are some rather capable people on this team. Take that Günther — somewhat impractical, but dispenses a lot of useful knowledge. Else, the Swede, she's really nice, forward-looking, no cold feet. You can tell by the way she interrupted Günther during his comprehensive presentation. And Roger, the Englishman, he likes him, too. Arrogant, yes, but a straight arrow. He can't really figure out Carlos and Giulio, though. They seem relaxed, obviously have been acquainted for a long time, but you never know exactly where they stand. The one he has to keep an eye on is Jean-Jacques. He talks like a visionary, but his intellectual approach makes him inscrutable.

Jan-Hein considers giving Annette a quick call to keep her up to date, but decides to read the paper instead. Tomorrow is another day.

Akihiro Yamada clicks shut his Japanese translation computer. During the meeting he had jotted down some words that escaped him. But looking them up now didn't do much good. Words like *cul de sac* only added to his confusion.

He had experienced an odd day. His English was sufficient, so that wasn't the reason why he got lost in the ongoing discussions during today's meeting. Having worked in the United States for two years, he believed he understood Westerners quite well by now. But what had happened today was very strange. What the heck was everyone's problem?

Maybe it would be best to just wait and see how things turn out, he contemplates. It is a relaxing thought. Signaling from his table at Kobe restaurant, he asks his waiter to bring him the bill.

# 2

# Beyond Mars and Venus

*On cultural identity*

Although the EmLog meeting in the previous chapter is an imaginary case, anyone working in an international setting will have experienced similar interactions as those we just witnessed among the team members Rick, Jean-Jacques, Günther, Jan-Hein, and Akihiro. Their behavior is affected by their cultures.

Faced with the task of designing a model that explains work-related behavior in different cultures, I immediately wind up with a culturally determined problem. Will people from different cultural backgrounds be able to recognize the cultural preferences I described? And will everyone adhere to the same significance to the names and classifications I use, given the fact that I, too, am a product of my own culture? Don't we all give meaning to social observations according to our own worldview, our own personal preferences, biased by our own cultural framework? So how objective can a model be if culture leads to inevitably subjective interpretations?

To be sure, the terms that I use in my model are universally recognized. I will create common ground by starting this book with a look at an institution familiar to all cultures, the family.[5] The family — formerly the clan — is the archetype of culture. Everywhere in the world, people first learn about culture in the family they belong to. Every family applies specific norms and values, internally and to the world around them, every family has its own culture. Remember how your parents would tell you to behave yourself when visiting another family, reminding you that not every family did things the way yours did? What they were telling you, in essence, was that every family culture is different.

## Definition of Culture

Before we further analyze family life to discover its cultural elements, we have to reflect on what we mean by "culture." In a culture, a group of people attribute significance and weight to certain behaviors. Therefore, I define culture as a group's set of shared norms and values, expressed in the behavior of the group members. Hence, culture is never an objective standard for behavior, but involves accepting various individuals' convictions and opinions.

Since I confine myself to work-related cultural elements, I will only bring up aspects of national cultures insofar as they influence management styles, ways of organizing, communicating, or cooperating. Of course, a nation can host many subcultures: urban or rural, state, district, or city. For inhabitants of a country these cultural

---

[5]Either nuclear or extended, including live-in family members, such as grandmothers, grandfathers, uncles, or aunts.

differences are quite meaningful, but outsiders are more aware of the similarities than of the differences, especially upon a first visit or brief stay. That is why I confine the model to the differences between national cultures. It does not deal with cultural differences within a country.

When discussing national culture in this book, I mean the culture of the majority or of a dominant portion of people in the country. So when I talk about "the American management style," I don't mean to generalize that "all Americans have this management style." I am simply referring to a style that many people identify as characteristic for Americans and not for other nationalities. In other words, work-related national culture is one which is preferred by a dominant group in only that specific country.

## Authority

Now let us turn to the family, which can be viewed as an archetype for team culture. Which principles are the bases for family relationships? In other words, how are families structured as a team?

Fundamentally, in all cultures the father and the mother have authority over their children. This is "natural" on account of their supposed experience, knowledge of the world, and access to financial resources. They do not need to prove their position, it is ascribed to them. Being parents implies "having authority over children." All parents in all cultures have an ascribed status on which they found their authority. In the family team, parents are the leaders.

We have just put our finger on a very important element of culture: ascribed authority.

Do other types of authority exist, then? Suppose our family consists of father, mother, son, and daughter. And a PC. One day Father catches a virus in his e-mail, and all his files are about to be deleted.

Fortunately, his daughter, Laura, is a computer whiz kid. She gives her father precise instructions, and, lo and behold, she solves the problem.

Father carefully followed the advice of his youngest child. Why? Where did Laura get this authority from? The answer: expertise. Now, expertise is always something that you have to be able to prove. Your status is achieved (not ascribed), and so is your authority. Laura has authority based on achieved status. She has to prove herself. If she fails, she loses her authority.

All cultures appear to recognize both ascribed authority and achieved authority. The essential difference between them is that people with ascribed status do not much like to be challenged to

---

## Gandhi and Hitler

At the occasion of Independence Day, 15 August, 2005, the Indian newspaper *Daily News and Analysis* asked some young people what freedom means to them. Rakesh, 21, answered, "My icon of freedom is my father, because all the freedom I have enjoyed until now is his gift to me."

Tejas, also 21, replied, "When I think of freedom, I automatically think of power, because there can be no freedom without someone powerful enough to give it to you. So, while I would say Mahatma Gandhi, Adolf Hitler also springs to mind."

I found these answers striking, because these youngsters clearly perceive freedom as a gift from an ascribed authority ("my father gave it to me"), and this ascribed authority can be good or bad (Gandhi or Hitler).

In cultures in which authority is based on achievement, people generally feel that you have a right to be free, and that you can create freedom.

---

18

prove their authority. They'll most likely interpret any questioning of their authority as an insult. People with achieved status, on the other hand, are used to being challenged. As long as your arguments are valid, you can disagree with them without getting into serious trouble. The authority coming from achieved status is also limited to the field in which the person is successful, whereas the authority of ascribed status goes beyond a person's work and stays with him in other social relations.

However, not all cultures attach the same importance to both kinds of authority. As we shall see in the following chapters, a cultural preference for one of these two types of authority is of great importance for the effectiveness of a leadership style. Leaders with an ascribed authority have difficulty in dealing with people who argue with them, whereas leaders with an achieved authority are more apt to discuss their decisions. If you are unaware of the kind of leader heading your team or organization, you can easily get into trouble.

## Rules

Exploring the family as an archetype a bit further, we discover, apart from authority, another element that is recognizable to all cultures: rules.

If a family usually has dinner at 7 PM, the rule makes sense that everyone should be home in time. Suppose son Martin one day comes home twenty minutes late. One way to deal with the rule is that, say, Mother tells Martin, "You are late, you broke the rule, you will be punished." And if Martin dares to resist with, "Yes, but . . . ," she curtly replies, "No excuses."

Or, Father could ask Martin why he is late. Martin answers that it started raining when he was on the verge of leaving his friend's house, and he decided to wait because he did not bring a coat. Father accepts his explanation, and tells Martin to call home when something like this happens again.

There is a fundamental difference between the way these parents deal with rules. Mother might as well put up a short list of rules in the kitchen. Any deviation from these rules will be perceived as a mistake that may be punished. This method clears the way for quick decisions because most situations are easy to judge. Father's point of reference is more complicated. He allows exceptions to the rules; he deliberates upon the circumstances of each transgression. His judgment depends on the context. He needs to analyze the details of the situation, which obviously takes more time.

These ways of dealing with rules constitute two distinct systems. One strives for rules with a universal validity, independent of context, resulting in black and white orders, whereas the other considers the circumstances that might allow exceptions to the rules. The latter system can become quite complex if one feels the need to record every exception. A culture with a preference for universal rules can be very decisive. A culture with a preference for context-dependent rules will take more time for decision making.

We can notice that some cultures value decisiveness, and thus prefer as few rules as possible. Other cultures, however, look upon decisiveness in complex situations as very suspicious, and are not bothered by myriad rules. Just look at the way the European Union regulations are perceived in different cultures. The British traditionally oppose Brussels' passion for regulations. The British do not see a need for detailed regulations, but whenever a rule is established they take it very seriously. So if Brussels enacts new rules and regulations, the British are of the opinion that they should be obeyed. On the other hand, countries like Portugal, Spain, or Greece are quite stoic about EU regulations. Their attitude is that time will tell how much room there is for exceptions, or maybe even suspensions. Needless to say, the British can barely come to terms with this approach.

## Individual Freedom

We have now identified two strongly regulating forces in the family, recognizable by all cultures: <u>authority and rules</u>. <u>Authority can be ascribed or achieved</u>. <u>Rules (laws and procedures)</u> can be perceived

---

### Restriction versus Insecurity

The perception of freedom is culturally determined. I found a striking example of this in a *New York Times* article. The author expressed his aversion to the huge fines doled out in the Asian city-state Singapore for dropping a cigarette butt or possessing chewing gum. The American journal depicted this state as extremely un-free because of its over-regulation and "Big Brother is watching you" features. In a letter to the editor, a Singaporean reader delicately pointed out that in his city people can safely walk any street at night, while you may risk your life if you do so only two blocks away from the New York Times building.

This example shows that to Americans, freedom means arranging your life in the way you prefer, whereas Singaporeans experience freedom as being free from worries, feeling protected against social threats, thanks to a shared responsibility.[6] In other words, what can be experienced as freedom by an American can be felt as insecurity by a Singaporean. And what a Singaporean may call freedom may be called restrictive by an American.

---

[6]In Abraham Maslow's Hierarchy of Needs theory, self-actualization is the final goal, and safety is a lower need. Apparently this is true for Western societies, but not so much for some Asian societies.

as universally applicable, resulting in a simple system, or context-dependent with a focus on exceptions, resulting in a complex system.

These forces influence people's behavior. They let themselves be restricted by rules and the orders handed down by authority figures. The absence of these two regulating forces would allow a greater freedom of behavior, but would also provoke an ongoing battle between individuals, resulting in the survival of the fittest. That is why people feel comfortable with restrictions; they guarantee a certain degree of security and protect against chaos. Hence, they allow for individual freedom.

## Individuality and Role Behavior

We have discussed the culturally determined behavior of the individual, but not the individual itself. Coming back to the family, we observe that all family members make a distinction between themselves and the other members. They can all speak about "I"; I differ from you, this is what I want, what I can do and what I love, I have the right to disagree with you. That "I" is determined by character, taste, and talents. Individuality means thinking in terms of "I," without obligations to others.

By defining someone's individuality, have we also defined someone's identity? One day Martin is playing basketball with his friends. He is passionate about this sport. Nevertheless, chances are good that he will interrupt his game if he sees Laura fall off her bike and hurt herself. He will sacrifice his favorite activity ("this is what I prefer to do right now") to help his sister ("I feel morally obliged to help"). Martin does not want to see himself as an egoist who neglects his little sister with a bleeding knee. That is just not the kind of person he is. In other words, our identity does not only consist of our individuality, independent of others, but also consists of the role we choose in relation to others. For some people, identity will be primarily shaped by individuality — the need to be different. Others feel identity more as the way they relate to other people — their specific role in the community. A creative artist is more on the individual side of the individuality-role behavior axis. But a police officer tends to identify himself with his role in the community (wearing a uniform in itself symbolizes conformism and role behavior). The former accentuates its rights, the latter its obligations and duties.

## Different but Similar

Young people often want to be noticed as unique, different, sometimes even eye-catching. They show off, their behavior screaming "Look at me!" At the same time they are pure conformists when it comes to dress code, gadgets, or music. More than in any later stage of their life, they want to be seen as identical to their friends.

This need to fit in with the group chokes young people's individuality. Sometimes a group starts operating as if it were one person. Both behavior and responsibility are shared, so group behavior can get out of hand because nobody really feels responsible for his or her behavior. In Western countries, maturity tends to coincide with the expansion of a sense of individual responsibility and the break away from conformism.

If Westerners meet cultures that show a strong group orientation, expressed by a reluctance to take personal responsibility and a preference for conformist and formal behavior, they tend to relate this to the negative aspects of Western group behavior. However, this interpretation is totally inadequate.

These same differences can be found in national cultures. Some societies stress individuality, while others value role behavior. In individualistic societies, freedom is supreme, although it can come with insecurity. In role-orientated societies, freedom is based on security.

## Universal Aspects of Culture

By analyzing the structure and behavior of a family, we have pinned down a couple of universal aspects of culture: authority, based on ascribed and achieved status; rules, forming simple or complex systems; and identity, built up of individuality and role behavior. All cultures recognize these aspects. Although cultures appreciate them differently, everyone understands which values are at stake.

Groups of people share preferences, which they make their standards. That behavior gets normative power (this is "normal"), and other people start acting accordingly. This is how we come to culturally determine behavior.

We encounter cultural differences at all levels, be it in a family, a profession, a team, an organization, or an entire nation. It is these universal aspects of cultural characteristics, as identified in the family — authority, rule systems, individuality, and role behavior — that are the basis for the culture model I have named the Model of Freedom.

# 3

# The Model of Freedom

*On the cultural model*

**EmLog Worldwide:**
After apologizing to his son for not picking him up from basketball practice, Rick Delano sits down with his wife and buddy, Alice. They have gone through high seas together, both family-wise and career-wise. With her he can unburden his heart, and that is what he really needs at the moment. "Alice, it's an incredible bunch I met today. You wouldn't believe it, but the way these Europeans tackle a new challenge, it's amazing! Imagine the chances lying ahead for them. But they act like they're being punished. Legal obstacles, practical obstacles, obstacles from the past, obstacles in the future, obstacles, obstacles, obstacles, enough obstacles to turn into stone."

"Rick," Alice interrupts, "you remember the Indian ICT guy you worked with back home? He called Europe a museum. Think about it."

Rick Delano is obviously bewildered by his first encounter with a European team, and luckily has a partner with whom he can let off some steam. He will, however, need some insight in cultural characteristics to be able to fend off this image of massive opposition and find ways to motivate his talented, but tough, bunch. He needs the Model of Freedom.

The Model of Freedom categorizes characteristic group behavior. It starts with a circle that stands for the entire range of possible human behavior. Then, to indicate specific behavior, we divide the circle into four parts on two axes, each part representing the aspects of culture that we discussed in Chapter 2: attitude toward authority, systems of rules, individuality, and role behavior in society. Depending on how much one values these cultural aspects, one scores high or low on the axes. By connecting the scores on all four aspects, we can create a diagram of culturally determined behavior. By comparing the diagrams of team members, teams, organizations, or even entire countries, we gain insight into their range of cultural styles and preferences, which enables us to adjust our behavior, decisions, and processes to best enhance our ability to cooperate with them.

Let's look at the Model of Freedom more closely, building it step by step.

## Individuality and Role Behavior

How do people express their identity? A person's identity is defined by her individuality (her character and talents) and by her attitude toward their role in society (the way she adjusts to others).

These two aspects of identity influence one's thinking and acting, and determine the first (horizontal) axis of the MoF.

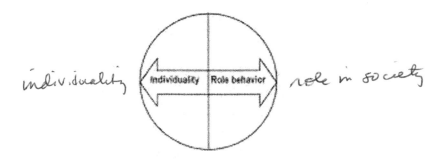

*In the left half of the circle we place all behavior that we can link with individuality, and in the right half of the circle we place all behavior that we can link with one's role in society.*

## Thinking and Acting

How does an individual express his or her identity? Through thoughts and actions. This fundamental division is traceable in "theory and practice," in "planning and implementing," in "process and action." This division determines the second (vertical) axis of the MoF.

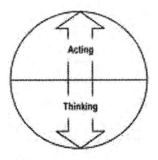

*In the top half of the circle we locate all human behavior that has to do with "acting." In the bottom half of the circle we locate all behavior that has to do with "thinking": theories, processes, rules and regulations, laws, and plans.*

# Authority

In analyzing the family, we found cultural elements that we can now fit into the MoF. People express their identity through their behavior, but they are not completely free to do so. They are limited by authorities.

As we've discussed, authority can be either ascribed or achieved. If a person's authority is based on what he *is*, his authority is founded on an ascribed status. He has authority "by nature," which is not to be challenged; others should adjust to it. If a person's authority is based on what he *does*, then that authority is achieved. His authority depends on how successful he is. This implies that he can lose this authority if he fails or if someone else is more successful.

We can depict this in the MoF as follows:

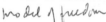

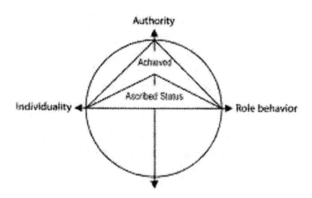

*The maximum score of behavior, influenced by authority with ascribed status, is represented in the small triangle. (The top lies halfway up the axis.) The further we move away from the center of the circle, the more we believe that authority can be challenged, that it has an achieved and defensible status.*

## What the Gurus Say about Power

Power turns out to be an important discriminating factor in all cultures. However, Fons Trompenaars does not distinguish Power as a dimension in his culture model.[7] Charles Hampden-Turner, Trompenaars' counterpart and author of *The Seven Cultures of Capitalism,* attempted to compensate this by introducing the dimension Equality versus Hierarchy. But this proposal did not make it in the Trompenaars school.

Geert Hofstede refers to the dimension Power Distance, the extent to which people accept differences in power. This term exclusively hints at power based on ascribed status.

But by using the dimension Authority (power based on ascribed or achieved status) instead of Power Distance, the MoF is able to explain why, for instance, American managers can exercise forceful power, but, according to Hofstede's research, still score relatively low on Power Distance. In fact, they score low on ascribed status. They do not feel any special respect for seniority or aristocracy. In the United States, what really grants status to a person — and ultimately power, much power — is youth, energy, decisiveness, achievements, and success. Hence, the United States scores high on Achieved Authority in the Model of Freedom.

---

[7]See Appendix 1: The Theories of Hofstede and Trompenaars.

## Systems of Rules

The other universally recognizable element we identified in the family is rules. Rules can either form a simple system or a complex system.

In the simple system, rules and regulations are static and cannot easily be discussed. Breaking a rule is wrong; diverging from the rule is hardly tolerated.

In the complex system, rules and regulations exist mainly to guide us. Deviating from the rules is acceptable if it can be supported by rational or emotional arguments. In complex systems it is perfectly all right to take some time to make a deliberate decision instead of automatically submitting to existing rules

In the MoF it looks like this.

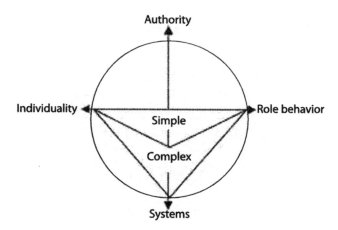

*Simple systems are supported by scores from the center of the circle to halfway down the axis. The further one moves away from the center, the more complex the systems become. Since complex systems allow flexibility in the interpretation of the rules, and people are not limited in their behavior by strict rules, we find the maximum score in freedom at the tip of the large upside-down triangle.*

## What the Gurus Say about Rules

Hofstede and Trompenaars deviate in how they deal with the second discriminating factor in cultures, systems of rules.

Regarding what he calls the dimension of Uncertainty Avoidance, Hofstede assumes that peoples' need for an extensive system of rules and regulations derives from uncertainty. Anglo-Saxon cultures, with their relatively low need for rules, would be less inclined to avoid uncertainty than, for instance, Latin cultures, which long for detailed rules and regulations. Hofstede argues that, because of their constant struggle against uncertainty, Latin people are more stressed and hence, more emotional than, for example, Anglo-Saxons.

Trompenaars' view is different. He draws a distinction between Universalist cultures, which strictly obey the rules and therefore do not need to establish many exceptions, and Particularist cultures, in which context affects how rules should be followed, and make a point of allowing for exceptions. According to Trompenaars, most Latin cultures are particularistic, whereas the United States is extremely universalistic.

My Model of Freedom reflects Trompenaars' view on rules. In my opinion, the density of rules does not hint at peoples' uncertainty, but at their wish to feel free to allow exceptions to the rules, since that is what complex issues ask for. Here we see two different perceptions of freedom. In one perception, freedom is guaranteed by a clear set of rules; you know your rights and duties. In the other perception, freedom means being able to apply exceptions to existing rules.

## Short but Meaningful

There is an anecdote about the poet Goethe, who supposedly wrote to a good friend, "Sorry to bother you with such a long letter, but today I had no time to write a short one."

Obviously, when writing this chapter I had time to keep it short, in order not to overload you with information at this early stage. The result is a very condensed introduction to the MoF. But the MoF contains many meaningful aspects that need elaboration. We will explore them in the next chapters.

# 4

# Perceptions of Reality

## *On cultural orientations*

**EmLog Worldwide:**

The American, Rick Delano, was assigned to implement a new standardized software system for all European EmLog branches. He convoked his team in Amsterdam for the kick-off. In his introduction, meant to energize the troops, he praised the entire team and showed them timetables and targets for the project. Thirty minutes, that's all it had taken him.

Then Günther Windesheim took the floor. The German had done a Herculean job of adapting the American software system to European standards. It was important preparatory work, for which he had had to call in legal experts. But his presentation had been so tedious and detailed that everyone had lost interest within half an hour.

After lunch Jean-Jacques Bauduin was supposed to explain how France was preparing for its role as the first European country to implement the new software. But instead of coming to the point, he started off with a lecture. He considered it of the utmost importance to shed light on the significance the new software system would have on the future of the entire automotive industry.

The international EmLog team is about to start running a new joint project. By watching their behavior, we can see that the team members have quite different perceptions of reality. At the end of this chapter, once the Model of Freedom is completely assembled, we will be able to recognize each of the four cultural orientations represented in the EmLog team.

## Action-orientation

People or cultures that prefer to focus on concrete actions can be depicted by the following diagram:

I call this an action-orientation. We find action-oriented national cultures predominantly in Anglo-Saxon countries like the United States, the United Kingdom, and Australia, but also in parts of South Africa.

### Features:
- Action-oriented people combine a preference for achieved authority with a need for simple systems of rules.

- They want to be decisive. They'd prefer to make a fast decision and risk failure than make a slow decision and risk being late. They shoot from the hip, and do not expect to have a hit at each shot; they can deal with failure.

- This hankering for speed in order to get results leads them to simplify circumstances by eliminating all redundancies, thus facilitating the decision-making process.

- They are <u>not</u> particularly interested in *how* <u>things work,</u> but in the fact *that* <u>they work.</u> They go for tangible and visible results.

- They have a strong drive to achieve, to raise the bar, to energize other people. This makes them future-oriented. Hence, in these cultures young and energetic people, who have a promising future ahead, are highly valued.

- The motto of action-oriented people might be: "If you really want it, get it."

## Outside Perception:

- Other cultures may be tempted to interpret the need for simplification as simplicity. However, this is a mistake. Action-oriented people do acknowledge the complexity of situations and issues, but strongly believe in distinguishing between <u>main issues (content) and side issues (context)</u>.

- The tendency to go for visible results and concrete outcomes is often judged as a tendency to ignore the "real" world, to not appreciate existing relationships or valuable experiences.

- The appreciation for a young and energetic appearance in action-oriented cultures contrasts with most Asian cultures that ascribe a high status to the aged.

- Decisiveness can be perceived as inflexibility. The reluctance to reopen a discussion once a decision is made does not allow much scope.

## Expressions:

- Carly Fiorina, former CEO of Hewlett Packard, once said in an interview, while talking about her education in medieval history and philosophy at Stanford University, "Every week we had to read a medieval philosophical book and summarize it in two pages. I found it very instructive, this training in finding the essence of a complex whole."[8] For people from a culture with a preference for complex rule systems this would make no sense; in fact, it would be a torment since for them there is no meaning without a complex context. Carly enjoyed looking for the essence, the truth that goes without exception, while other cultures believe that the truth depends on the context.

- In U.S.-based multinational organizations, an action-oriented measure like bringing the head count down (a visible intervention for the shareholders' benefit), is the kind that allows no exceptions for branches in single countries. For other cultures, this has no rationale. After all, if a branch has its own budget, it will often be forced to hire local temporary personnel at higher costs to fill the gap left by the eliminated staff. This is more expensive, but the head office doesn't mind as long as it does not show in the official head count. Likewise, a U.S. company that attempts to cut costs by issuing a rule to limit all air travel seems to be insensitive to the fact that traveling by car or train in Europe is often more expensive than buying airline tickets, thus raising the transportation costs for short distances for these branches.

- In organizations we can discern action-orientation in its least diluted form in sales departments. By definition, salespeople will assist their customers in making a decision by solely presenting the quintessence of an issue, and skipping matters of minor importance. For a salesperson, it's important to encourage customers to make fast decisions, to prevent them from shopping elsewhere. Too much information is distracting. Sales is the department with the strongest market orientation; they have an eye for what the customer wants or should want.

---

[8]Interview in *Management Team*, February 28, 2003.

## Process-orientation

People or cultures with a preferred <u>focus on thinking</u> (or on the abstract versus the concrete) can be depicted as follows:

I call this a process-orientation. We find process-oriented national cultures predominantly in Latin countries, and in an occasional Asian country.

### Features:

- Process-oriented people accept ascribed authority along with complex systems of rules.

- They are prepared to discuss and weigh an issue at length before taking action. In organizations, these people feel the need to be well prepared and to always have smart arguments on hand. They stress careful decision making in order to prevent mistakes, even if it is time-consuming.

- Time is seen as a necessary investment, since fast decisions are regarded as either unwise or unimportant.

- They value discussion and consultation, the consideration of all possible exceptions and valuable lessons from the past. They have an inclination to analyze issues and contextualize them. For them, this is the arena where they can shine; educational systems in these countries emphasize the skill to excel in intellectual debates.

- They are not only motivated by targets and goal-setting, but also by the intellectual process that leads to them.

- They are aware of their place in the hierarchy. Their actions will always be confined to what their superiors permit.

- Conflicts are undesirable. If hierarchy does not solve the issue, all diplomatic talents will be deployed for reconciliation.

- No shooting from the hip! They should only shoot after taking careful aim. And because they take a long time to aim, they feel stupid if they miss.

- They tend to identify themselves more with the imperceptible processes than with the tangible results. In other words, the *how* and *why* are more important than the final result.

- Life is a complex process, if not an art; *Savoir vivre*, could be their motto.

## Outside Perception:

- Their reliance on hierarchical structures and their refusal to accept individual responsibility at staff level is seen as fostering authoritarian leadership styles.

- Non–process-oriented cultures fear delays when process-oriented individuals work within a matrix structure in which they work with more than one boss on a project team.

- Outsiders perceive long decision-making procedures as unnecessary and irritating.

- Management styles such as delegating, management by objectives, and empowerment can fall completely flat if they are implemented without considering a process-oriented culture's preference for ascribed authority.

## Expressions:

- The tendency to adjust to context and to consider possible exceptions and past experiences leads to a great sensitivity to subtleties and details. Depending on the scores on Individuality (Latin countries) or Role behavior (Asian countries), this contributes to the cultural environment for design and creation respectively, or control and quality products. A good example of a combination of design and quality can be found in one of the rare successful joint ventures in the car industry, that of Renault and Nissan.

- We can see the differences between an action-oriented and a process-oriented culture by looking at the experiences of a Boston-based consulting firm in Europe. This firm executed a pilot project for the British branch of an American paper products company, leading to an improved production process. In the United Kingdom the firm had worked with the line supervisor and his team, asking questions about stocks, the distance to raw material, changing times of tools in the production line, and so on. This information was the base for the final changes that were eventually implemented. The consulting firm was instantly asked to repeat this successful strategy for the Spanish branch. But it did not work out the same way. The Spanish manager reported a delay in the delivery of adapted cutting tools, more time was needed, and so on. It took months to get half the changes implemented, and some just never happened. How come? In the U.K. the boss, with his achieved status, did not feel that his position was threatened; his people were empowered. But in Spain the boss' status was based on ascription; he felt a need to be indispensable and in control. At the end of the day, wasn't he responsible for the outcome? Now the consulting firm had bypassed him by dealing directly with his subordinates. What was in it for him, if he cooperated? He could only lose.

- Do not expect a quick fix if you want to do business with, for instance, a Mexican. A task-oriented person might be tempted to arrange a short meeting at the airport to efficiently bridge the gap between two flights. Her Mexican counterpart will agree to such an arrangement, and he will probably show up, but he will utilize the meeting to get acquainted in a process-oriented way. So the conversation may be about the beauty of his hometown with its grand cathedral—and, by the way, you are invited to come along and see it with your own eyes next visit! The conversation might turn to all kinds of topics, but not straightaway to the business that lies ahead. That will have to come at the next meeting, or the one after that.

# Task-orientation

The third and fourth cultural orientations, "task-orientation" and "role-orientation," cover respectively the left and right half of the circle. This expresses that they both show aspects of "action" and "process."

People or cultures with a strong focus on individuality will be depicted like this:

I call this a task-orientation. Task-oriented national cultures are predominantly found in the northern European countries.

## Features:
- It is the task that defines their relationship with others. Just like action-oriented cultures, task-oriented cultures prefer achieved authority, but, more than action-oriented cultures, they are inclined to consider the context of issues and exceptions to the rules.

- Their high score on individuality and their focus on fulfilling a common task influence their ways of communicating and discussion — a very direct style, not bothered by formalities, procedures, or regulations. They will always try to make perfectly clear where they stand.

- When cooperating in teams, they hold on to their personal sense of responsibility, which is linked to certain rights, like the right to have access to information, and the right to give negative feedback.

- The task-oriented team leader is a *primes inter pares,* the first among its equals.

- They don't trust heroes; every individual has the right to be different, but not the right to claim superiority.

- Everyone is personally responsible for his or her deeds and should be reminded of that.

- "Be critical whenever necessary," could be the motto of task-oriented people.

## Outside Perception:

- Their directness is easily perceived as bluntness, which is not appreciated in many cultures.

- Since they are used to communicating directly with their superiors, they appear to have no respect for authority.

- Non–task-oriented cultures can have a hard time dealing with this culture's initially critical or negative approach to proposals or target-settings.

- Their criticism can be taken for personal antipathy. This is undeserved, since task-oriented people are apt to dismiss any feelings of personal sympathy or antipathy when working on a common task.

- They can be perceived as too talkative and too fond of meetings ("more talking than walking"), because their attempts to strive for equality means they do a lot of information sharing.

- They are considered difficult to motivate, since they do not go for outstanding behavior (heroism), and thus cannot be rewarded with visible signs of superiority like a special parking place or a celebration in which they are applauded by their colleagues. They are more motivated by incentives like a higher salary or extra holidays.

## Expressions:

- Action-oriented concepts like "Employee of the Month" or "Salesman of the Quarter" evoke embarrassment rather than pride. If McDonald's introduces the Best Employee of the Month incentive, "rewarding" people by posing their picture on a plaque in the restaurant, it will have a reverse effect in a country like the Netherlands. Dutch employees will try hard not to be the best employee of the month.

- Task-oriented people typically express "judging" opinions, like, "That was stupid of you to have missed my presentation . . ." and "Heavens, what did you do to your hair . . . ?" But they don't mean for you to take it personally.

- They respect a strict division between work and private time. Many are 9 to 5 people who don't appreciate work-related calls after office hours and are reluctant to socialize with colleagues. New colleagues, even if they come from abroad and have not yet found their own circle of friends, will seldom be invited for a drink after work.

# Role-Orientation

People or cultures who emphasize the community aspects of working together will be depicted by the following diagram:

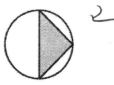

I call this a role-orientation. National role-oriented cultures are found in most Asian and some African countries.

## Features:

- They combine a high score on role behavior with a preference for ascribed authority.[9]

- They need to have a clear role on a team and formalized relations and responsibilities.

- They are always aware of the role they have to fulfill and its accompanying duties. They conform to their role, and thus hand in part of their individual accountability. This leads to disciplined behavior combined with the desire to excel in that role.

- It is not individual strength that motivates them, but the strength of the team they participate in.

- Their low score on individuality expresses that they are not inclined to address their individual needs and do not feel the urge to express

---

[9]In national role-oriented cultures, we never found role behavior combined with achieved status. It just seems not to exist in the countries we analyzed. We do, however, find role behavior linked to achieved status in self-steering teams in organizations.

divergent opinions, although they have them as much as anybody else in any culture.

- The low score on individuality is also the base of perfection in role-oriented cultures that consider a team member's deviating opinions or obstinacy a hindrance to quality or discipline.

- Conflicts disrupt this role, jeopardize the task, and should therefore be avoided. This calls for a formal, indirect style of communication, courteous, free from blunt refusals. "Yes" or "maybe" are frequently used, when "no" is meant.

- The motto for role-oriented people could be, "Always avoid confrontation."

## Outside Perception:

- They are inflexible toward change because change allows for unpredictability, which threatens their role definition and thus the quality of their performances.

- Their conformity is often considered inefficient. Their drive to follow the rules without looking for solutions that might go better, faster, or might be more appropriate can be a hard-to-swallow attitude for especially action- or task-oriented people.

- Because of their indirect speech and their urge to prevent conflicts, often accompanied by a smile, they come across as very friendly. But the smile may hide feelings of discomfort.

- The indirect speech and the urge to prevent conflicts can also make it very difficult to get access to the information you are looking for.

- You'll seldom deal with only one member of a role culture. Very often you'll see people present in the conference room and have no idea why they are in the meeting.

## Expressions:

- I once watched a team of three Sri Lankan cleaners scrub the marble tiles of a staircase in a hotel (a job that would have been assigned to one single person in a task-oriented culture). One scrubbed really hard. His brush did not leave any corner untouched. Another poured water, splashing many buckets of water for the third cleaner to mop. All had their specific role. They would not touch each other's tool. In the end the stairs were declared clean, but with three pairs of bare feet running up and down they were not spotless. This story demonstrates how once a role-oriented person's role is defined, the result of his work is judged a success, if everybody did what he or she had to do. No proof is needed. Any argument from outsiders about inefficiency or a poor result will be met with astonishment.

- Whoever enters a restaurant or a bank in Japan will be greeted courteously by the entire staff, giving the customer the impression of a very warm welcome. But nothing personal is meant. It is a ritual attitude toward you as a customer (your role), not toward you as a person.

- In China, team members communicate more with their superiors than with their fellow team members, (ascribed leaders want reports and make the decisions) to the extent that people enter the office and start working without so much as greeting their colleagues. I have met many Chinese members of international teams who expressed their initial amazement about a working environment that wants them to chat about the weather or inquire about one's children. Some told me that even saying "good morning" was completely unnecessary and uncomfortable.

## Meals: Savor or Devour

Cultural orientations are also expressed in eating habits.

Action-oriented cultures promote quick bites, whereas process-oriented cultures are associated with good wine, a delicate sauce, and a dessert. Just compare a lunch in the United States with an average lunch in southern Europe. Getting a hamburger in a fast-food restaurant means enjoying action, speed — you do not even have to get out of your car. Pour some ketchup on, chew six times, swallow, and off you go to your next appointment. A lunch in southern Europe takes place at the dinner table, with real napkins. Along with wine, people choose their favorite mineral water. After the salad and the freshly baked fish, lunch is concluded with your choice of several cheeses. Lunch conversation is often about food. People revel in their sophisticated knowledge, taste, and personality. It is the process itself that is being savored.

Northern Europeans, typically task-orientated, do not have a special appetite for lunch. A sandwich, a glass of milk, and an apple will do, as long as the meal is nourishing and healthy. And, by the way, you are supposed to finish your plate.

In role-oriented cultures all dishes are served at the same time, and the tastes are well-tuned: something sweet, something salty, something bitter, something sour. The tastes are as varied as the crockery. From India to Japan, people enjoy the pure taste of every separate bite. All dishes have a role that contributes to the final aim: enjoying the process of satisfying your appetite.

## Application of Diagrams

All national cultures can be categorized by one of the four orientations comprising the MoF. Having discerned that many Latin countries have a process-oriented culture, the Anglo-Saxon countries an action-oriented culture, Northern European countries a task-oriented culture, and many Asian countries a role-oriented culture,[10] the question is how do we apply this knowledge.

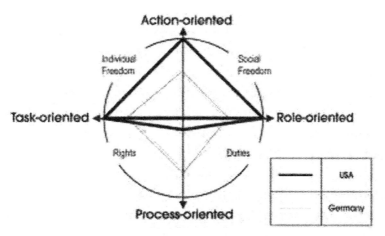

*The United States are strongly action-oriented. Germany differs somewhat from the task-oriented Northern European countries in the sense that it has some characteristics of a process-orientation.[11] Delano's and Windesheim's diagrams do not have much in common, which means that their preferences for leadership or communication styles are deviating. Delano is good at delegating, expects initiatives, and is very decisive. Windesheim expects clear orders, tends to frequently report back to his boss, and prospers in a working environment where long-term decisions are deliberated at length.*

---

[10]Due to a lack of reliable management data, I am not able to categorize the various African cultures.

[11]The diagrams are based on scores originating from the Appreciative Inquiry method, described in the Introduction. For a justification, see Appendix 2.

The MoF allows us to depict different cultural orientations in a diagram. Comparing these diagrams offers insight into the points of difference and similarities among these cultures, and thus delivers a key to what you would like to understand in the professional behavior of people from other cultures.

To illustrate this, refer to the diagram on page 47, which compares the national cultural orientation of the American, Rick Delano, with that of the German, Günther Windesheim.

## Culture Is Emotion

When people from different cultural orientations have a discussion, they should realize that emotions can easily overrule the ratio especially between action- and process-oriented people. Emotions can cause a situation to hit the fan.

In organizations, action-oriented people are not afraid of making mistakes, and they pragmatically adapt to ongoing operations. They do not fancy long preparations, but prefer clear milestones to pave their way. Little priority goes to invisible or intangible issues. That is why shareholders in action-oriented cultures do not reward a company's investment in general maintenance; they'd rather see it buy gleaming new machinery.

Process-oriented people, on the other hand, painstakingly try to avoid mistakes. They feel at ease with detailed preparation and planning, with clearly ascribed responsibilities. This, by the way, is not a guarantee for a smooth operation. On the contrary, the resulting complexity frequently causes the opposite, necessitating process-oriented people to come up with creative and pragmatic interventions.

Cultures with an action-orientation risk being accused of black-and-white thinking, of oversimplifying matters, of only valuing the result. Cultures with a process-orientation, on the other hand, are easily blamed for spending a lot of time coming up with unclear decisions.

# Warning

Although individuals within the same cultural orientation show many similarities in their behavior, the depiction of national cultures in the MoF is somewhat stereotyped. Since individual persons attach slightly different significances to the values represented in the MoF, every human being will have a unique diagram.

## MBTI and the Model of Freedom

The Myers-Briggs Type Indicator (MBTI) was originally designed as a sorting and awareness instrument, just like the MoF.

MBTI differentiates personal preferences on four scales, resulting in sixteen personality types. The scales are: Extroversion-Introversion (E versus I), Sensing-Intuition (S versus N), Thinking-Feeling (T versus F), Judging-Perceiving (J versus P).

Although the MBTI was not designed as a test or a recruitment and selection tool, that has become its common application nowadays. Up to two million North Americans get MBTI-typed each year, and in some organizations people know each other by their MB-type. This is

(*cont.*)

not surprising in an action-oriented culture: what else could sorting be useful for, if not for benchmarking and competition?

However, MBTI appears not to be culturally neutral. It does not show similar distributions of types in different national cultures. Action-oriented cultures clearly prefer the personality features ESTJ (extrovert, sensing, thinking, judging); introvert types are generally seen as "troublesome" for an organization. That is because in action-oriented cultures people are raised to be communicative, sociable, and candid. Being extroverted is highly appreciated.

The INFP-type (introvert, intuitive, feeling, perceiving) is more common in role- and process-oriented cultures, where people may find it very challenging to work with extrovert and judging types. The Japanese, for example, have a saying: "Only dead fish have their mouth open."

The lesson we can learn from this is that each culture has its own frame of reference for what it considers to be introvert, extrovert, and the like, and how it is valued.

We should be careful to apply the action- or task-oriented cultural view across cultures if we want to fully use the added value of diverse approaches.

It's also important to stress that there is no value attached to any particular division of cultural orientations. No orientation out-classes another one. Each cultural orientation has developed within its own domain the most effective way of organizing things. It is when different cultural orientations meet and cooperate that challenges can arise, necessitating improved cultural intelligence.

# 5

# Paterfamilias or Superman

## *On leadership*

**EmLog Worldwide:**

Jean-Jacques Bauduin pops open his laptop and starts looking for an Internet connection in his hotel room. He feels better after his telephone conversation with his boss in Paris, in which he discussed what went on in today's project meeting.

What worried Jean-Jacques was that the American team leader, Rick Delano, had slapped him on the back, saying, "You decide what to do, Jean-Jacques. You know the French better than I do!" That man had absolutely no idea how things worked in France. He didn't realize that Jean-Jacques had no authority to order other people around. Jean-Jacques would be absolutely powerless without the backing — and quite some pressure — from the big chief in Chicago.

But Jean-Jacques had been hesitant to contradict Delano without first consulting with his superior in Paris. Fortunately, Paris shared Jean-Jacques' view that the American team leader could very well distribute tasks, but should not pass on the responsibilities. "For the time being," his boss had cheerfully advised, "just tell the American what he apparently wants to hear. We'll see how things work out later."

Management styles are very personal, strongly determined by character, experience, and talents. Nevertheless, cultural background can have a decisive influence. In all four cultural orientations, people have different opinions on what makes a good leader. The key to understanding these differences lies in the distinction between ascribed or achieved authority.

If a culture attributes great importance to ascribed authority — and thus values more who you are than what you do — a good leader is someone who studied at the right university, is the right age, masters the right language or, in some countries, belongs to the right class or dynasty.

If, on the other hand, a culture has more respect for achieved authority, a good leader will be someone with a dynamic style who pursues spectacular successes. Managers are as good as their last performance.

A manager with ascribed authority will not easily be asked to resign when she doesn't meet her company's expectations. However, a manager with achieved authority will have a hard time whenever concrete successes remain elusive for too long.

## Leadership Attributes

Most organizations differentiate between leadership and management. "Leadership" is about the future of the organization. "Management" is about the present, about keeping things under control, about solving ongoing problems.

Numerous companies are on the search for management assessment tools meant to turn their managers into leaders. Irrespective of their nationality — the American company 3M, the British-Dutch company Unilever, or the Japanese company Nissan — they have all introduced management development programs designed to develop leadership attributes. Ironically, it turns out that successful top business leaders, subjected to management assessments, often do not score high in all of the theoretically required attributes.

## Holy Men and Heroes

Leaders motivate people, but not everybody is motivated by the same incentives. Both religion and culture influence motivation systems.

Usually, people are motivated by rewarding the desired behavior. Most cultures value tangible rewards. A special parking place, a larger company car, or a cap in a special color can go a long way.

In some cultures, however, people do not want to stand out visibly. They would rather not be a public hero. This attitude is quite common in task-oriented cultures dominant in European countries that are influenced by Calvinism and similar protestant religions. Calvinism rejects saints or heroes. Modesty is what makes a person heroic. A public hero is regarded with some suspicion.

In contrast to these cultures of modest heroes are cultures that create heroes out of minor events. Here, heroes are outstanding people. They are a source of inspiration and motivation because they are the living proof that complex issues or dangerous situations can be solved by clear-cut decisions and actions. A strong call for heroism is found in most action-oriented cultures.

However, there is one attribute that is absolutely indispensable to be a successful leader. Every culture may have its own word for it, but it comes down to the quality of being able to motivate people: charisma.

## Charisma

Charismatic leadership is in vogue nowadays, but the concept has always existed. In the nineteenth century, the German sociologist Max Weber[12] distinguished the charismatic leader as one of three types of authority, the other two being the bureaucratic and the traditional leader. This typology could, in his opinion, also apply to commercial organizations. Weber's bureaucratic leader is in command because of his knowledge and his position in the hierarchy. In other words, he is a manager. Weber's traditional leader enjoys an ascribed status. He deserves the loyalty of his subordinates; he is entitled to privileges, and knows his ways in diplomacy and company politics.

A charismatic leader has the right personality and talents to make him a hero. Nietzsche called him Uebermensch; the Americans call him Superman. He has what it takes to generate change because he possesses special powers, he is future-oriented, he creates new values and new goals.

Charisma emerges in different forms, but it definitely consists of qualities which organizations believe can be acquired by managers. A charismatic leader embodies objectives that transcend organizational goals. He communicates high expectations for the performance of his people, and shows confidence in their ability to meet these expectations.

---

[12]Max Weber (1864–1920), *The Theory of Social and Economic Organization,* The Free Press, New York, 1947.

## What the Gurus Say about Successful Leaders

Fons Trompenaars and Charles Hampden-Turner do not use charisma as a starting point for successful leadership,[13] but the ability to deal with dilemmas. They analyze a management situation and isolate two apparently contradicting aspects. They have noted that instead of working toward a compromise between these two aspects, the successful leader will try to reconcile them.

Describing and reconciling dilemmas has become a popular problem-solving method.[14] It is an approach that can be traced back to the dialectic methods of thinkers like Plato, Hegel, and even Marx.

The ability to recognize and reconcile dilemmas is an important quality for modern leaders. But any free social being solves the dilemma of individuality (the right to be different) versus society (adapting to others) every second of his life. People who do not succeed in reconciling these two elements of identity are trying to compromise between rights and duties. They end up in situations where they feel they have lost something instead of gained something.

That is what charismatic leaders like Mahatma Gandhi, Winston Churchill, John F. Kennedy, and Mother Theresa had in common: a passion for a goal, dedication, vision, courage, and an energizing way of communicating.

---

[13]Trompenaars speaks of "innovative leadership" in *21 Leaders for the 21st Century*, Capstone, Oxford, 2001.
[14]I have also applied the method of reconciling dilemmas in my book *The Profit of Peace: Corporate Responsibility in Conflict Regions*, Greenleaf Publishers, London, 2005.

## Charismatic Leaders in Different Cultures

*Action-oriented cultures* are motivated by charismatic leaders with an achieved status. "This man/woman has really made it. Let's listen to him/her, because this person will lead us to success." Vision and courage are more important than control and protection. These leaders *sell* their decisions and energize their people by emphasizing tangible acts and short-term results. They inspire others to take risks, and to achieve innovations by pioneering. Many people may see Microsoft's CEO Bill Gates as charismatic. This type of leader can delegate responsibilities. Anything is possible until it shows to be impossible.

*Process-oriented cultures* expect a charismatic leader to be something in between a "paterfamilias" and an absolute ruler, a visionary who radiates self-confidence and at the same time does not forget to verify if his or her wishes are being fulfilled. Napoleon Bonaparte energized people, even after his first massive defeat. Offering protection and exercising control are the important ingredients of a charismatic leader in process-oriented cultures. People will arduously stand by this type of leader if they are assured of his or her support, since they know that ultimately he or she will carry all the responsibility. Therefore, delegating responsibility is only an option under strict conditions; the leader will tell people what he or she wants. Process-oriented cultures prefer Weber's traditional leadership style, which is based on ascribed status.

*Task-oriented cultures,* similar to action-oriented cultures, prefer leaders with an achieved status. But in these cultures a charismatic leader never really becomes a hero. They remain the *primus inter pares,* the perfect facilitator. They do not like selling or telling, they prefer to make suggestions. Reason dominates all arguments and discussions and should always refer to the task at hand. Charismatic leaders involve their people in the decision-making process and strive for consensus before eventually moving on to an independent decision. Keeping a low profile may result in garnering great admiration from others. In other words, charisma means modest leadership.

*Role-oriented cultures* place charismatic leaders on the top of the pyramid. There, they visibly have the most important role of all. Their position is founded on the ascribed status of an austere *paterfamilias*. They are permitted to use their power, and they should meet the expectations that people ascribe to their role. Even though they are powerful, their role also limits their power. Those role-boundaries should never be crossed. They are not allowed to change the system that they are part of. Thus, they guarantee stability, security, predictability. They will instruct, emphasizing duty. Role-oriented cultures, by definition, prefer Weber's bureaucratic leadership style.

---

### Three Japanese Warlords[15]

Many Japanese managers admire one of three historic personalities that symbolize three distinct management styles:

Tokugawa, a general from the Edo era, had a patient style. His methods are described by a popular poem: "The quiet bird — let us wait — until it sings."

Toyotomi, another warlord, believed in intervention: "The quiet bird — let us force it — to sing."

Oda, a military strategist and peacemaker: "The quiet bird — let us shoot it — before it can sing."

If we think about Akihiro Yamada, the Japanese team member at EmLog, and his reaction to Rick Delano's kick-off meeting, it is obvious that he adheres to the Tokugawa style.

---

[15]From: "Salary Man in Japan," JTB Inc., Japan, 1991.

## Leading an Intercultural Team

When leading an intercultural team, it is vital to reckon with the different cultural perceptions of good leadership.

Recognizing a different cultural preference is a first and important step. Working in an intercultural environment, therefore, starts with being aware of your own cultural influences, hard as it might be. Throughout your career as an international leader you will learn to refrain from taking your own style as a standard, and realize that there is no objective criterion for "right" behavior. When you no longer flatly disapprove of what you find awkward in someone else's behavior, no longer label someone's behavior as incompetent or unmotivated, you will show signs of a growing cultural intelligence.

Our imaginary EmLog case clearly illustrates the cultural difference between French and American expectations of leadership. In the MoF we can picture it as follows:

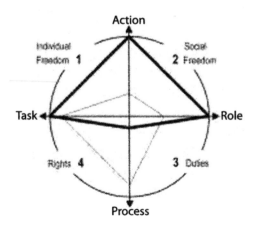

*The bold line stands for the way in which the American, Delano, leads; the thin line points out what the Frenchman, Bauduin, expects of a leader.*

Rick Delano scores high on achieved authority. His diagram covers a large surface of sector 1, which stands for individual freedom. Taking initiatives, being able to delegate, and empowerment are all part of this management style.

The diagram that represents Jean-Jacques Bauduin covers a much smaller surface of sector 1. His cultural preference is for a leader with ascribed authority, a manager who expects regular feedback, since he does not delegate responsibility. But Bauduin's diagram also reveals a high level of individuality, which means that he will try to escape from his boss's control whenever he gets the chance. The French call that *Système D*. The "D" stands for *débrouiller*, literally meaning to disentangle, to unravel, to untie, understood as "solve it your own way."

With regard to leadership styles, we can, for the moment, ignore the differences between the French and American diagrams in sectors 2 and 3. But sector 4 is significant, representing the need for rules that offer protection (defending somebody's rights). Bauduin's diagram covers a much larger surface of this sector than Delano's. This tells us that Bauduin does not feel protected by Delano, who, in his opinion, is careless and not empathic. The Frenchman suspects that the American will drop him if he fails to deliver instantly, since it is obvious that Delano does not share, but fully delegates, responsibility.

## Recognizing Differing Expectations

As stated earlier, the recognition that members of a team do have different expectations of leadership and are motivated by different qualities is an important condition for leaders, enabling them to improve their performance. But it is just the first step. Next comes the application of these insights in all phases of cooperation.

# 6

# Living with Barbarians

*On communication*

**EmLog Worldwide:**
Else Blomgard appreciated that Günther had worked through all those horrible European regulations, but after sixteen PowerPoint slides her head began to spin. And apparently the show was going to be on for another while longer. She interrupted Günther, asking for a handout to study at home. Her request upset him, she noticed. He blinked helplessly, but quickly recovered, and went on as if nothing had happened.

Her neighbor, Roger Lawson, who had impatiently been fiddling with his cell phone, took advantage of her interruption to leave the conference room. She could hear him making a call in the hallway. That was rude, she thought. But later that afternoon, when Jean-Jacques gave his highly philosophical presentation, she couldn't resist the urge to sneak away. Yamada seemed to be the only one who remained interested from start to finish.

The ancient Greeks called everyone who did not speak their language "Barbarians." The Romans adopted this habit and applied the word to all strangers. The North Africans call their mountain people the Berbers, Arabic for "Barbar." And the Europeans, until the late nineteenth century, called the entire north of Africa "Barbaria." The word "barbarian" originally stems from imitating the inarticulate language of "those strange people," babbling away. So, actually, it refers to unrefined language. When sharing the same language, people will not be considered barbarian. In the world of international organizations that language is English.[16] But though we all speak English, the way we express ourselves is still affected by our different cultures. In international settings, this can lead to painful misunderstandings.[17] In this chapter we will see how — with the help of some basic cultural intelligence — we can avoid that anything out of the ordinary inevitably leads to miscommunication.

## Content or Context

We've learned that the members of the intercultural EmLog team hold deviating opinions on what makes an effective presentation. The German, Günther, and the Frenchman, Jean-Jacques, treasure the complexity of complicated issues. However, their multifaceted presentations are a torture to the Swede and the Briton, who are anxious to get down to business.

---

[16]Surprisingly also called *lingua franca*, which originally means "Frankish tongue."
[17]For example, the British fondness for vague or surprising communication, *just for the fun of it*, can be hard for a non-native to grasp. Irony seems to be a cornerstone of British culture.

Process-oriented cultures have a strong urge to scrupulously consider the context of a subject or situation to make the essence of the message comprehensible. For them, "getting down to business" is not a matter of getting straight to the point, but rather taking the time to share an extensive line of thought with their audience, paying particular attention to relevant motives, history, and details. This is perceived as a lengthy and tedious process by people from an action-oriented culture, for whom the message itself is key; the context serves to fill in relevant details later.[18] Take Else, the Swede. She was satisfied knowing that she had access to research on European laws and regulations, thanks to Günther. She would look into the details later, when she needed them.

In some cultures, the context completely surmounts the content. The Japanese culture indicates this divergence with *honne* and *tatemae*. *Honne* means "from the heart" and refers to honestly meant messages. *Tatemae*, on the other hand, refers to statements, required by a specific social situation, which do not necessarily mirror one's true thoughts or feelings. It is the expression of the ultimate need to be polite and not confront people. Your audience is often supposed to understand what you really mean by the way you express yourself. The real message is in the process.

Those culturally determined communication styles can be found in all types of information exchanges, be it a PowerPoint presentation, a conference call, or an e-mail correspondence. People who rely upon a lot of context to get their message across are put at a disadvantage by all types of long-distance communication. After all, with today's speedy e-mails and phone calls, most context is lost, either

---

[18]Edward T. Hall made a distinction between communication styles with "high context" and "low context" in his classic *The Silent Language* (Doubleday, New York, 1959). These styles are dominant in, respectively, the process-/role-oriented and the action-/task-oriented cultures.

due to the conciseness or to the lack of non-verbal communication required in an era of few face-to-face meetings.

It can be tempting to reach for the "barbarian-reflex"; especially if communication becomes opaque, or in case of unpleasant feedback. But it is rather ineffective to look on a person as "strange" or "alien." If you want to communicate effectively on an intercultural level, you will have to invest in building trust. And trust is primarily built with information and communication. The more you get to know a stranger, the less you tend to look upon him or her as a barbarian. However, not all cultures build trust using the same kind of information.[19] That means one should be aware of one's own information needs and be able to recognize someone else's expectations.

## Information: Right or Privilege?

Cultural differences are not only expressed through communication styles, but also in the way people deal with information. To begin with: Who has access to information? Is it a right or a privilege to be informed by one's superiors? Is it considered necessary to exchange information with one's colleagues?

Managers in process- and role-oriented cultures do not feel the same need to share information as managers in task- and action-oriented cultures. Knowledge is power, and one does not share power (i.e., access to information) without getting something in return. Managers in process- and role-oriented cultures share their knowledge as late as possible, and then only on a need-to-know basis. Although they frequently ask for extensive information them-

---

[19]I will expand on this subject in Chapter 10.

selves, they reluctantly share information with their subordinates. Their position is partly determined by the fact that they are on the crossroad of information channels and, hence, in the position to exercise control. It is naïve to expect them to put this position in peril.

A Northern European company starting up production plants in China will soon discover that the communication between the Northern European, task-oriented project teams and the Chinese, role-oriented project teams will not proceed smoothly. In Northern Europe, as in Anglo-Saxon countries, team members advocate vivid exchanges of information. Channeling the information through the team leader is not wanted. Britons or Danes will easily ask their Chinese counterparts for information for their side of the project. In this case, multiple things can occur.

First possibility: no reply. Second possibility: the question is passed on to another colleague in China. Third possibility: an apparently irrelevant reply, by e-mail, because of the time lag. Any of these responses could be a result of the Chinese counterpart's embarrassment, since he or she does not feel in the position to reply. As a matter of fact, Chinese project teams pass almost all communication through their team leader. Team members only dispose of fragmented information that they will share exclusively with their superiors, not with colleagues. So, if Chinese managers receive a request for information, they will instantly wonder who this person is, and, above all, what his or her position in the hierarchy is. Besides, this person apparently expects the Chinese counterpart to dispose of that information, which is most probably not the case. The Chinese will try to cope with the situation without looking incompetent or stupid. Thus, delaying their response becomes an attractive option. Avoiding confrontation is always a priority in role-oriented cultures because confrontations can easily escalate, which is undesirable. Of course, these kinds of incidents are not beneficial to building mutual trust.

---

### Sparkling Teeth

Commercials and advertisements in different countries re-flect the way people prefer to be addressed, and the kind of information that entices them. Let me give you four ex-amples:

The Great Promise: A British commercial for toothpaste will emphasize the effect of the product. This is the result you will get if you use our toothpaste: sparkling, snow-white teeth between two cherry-red lips.

The Great Security: A German advertisement for the same product will show a man wearing a white medical coat, the expert, next to a flipchart showing the compo-nents of the toothpaste and its scientifically tested functions.

The Great Reassurance: A Spanish advertisement may use an authority — not a doctor or a technician as in Ger-many, but someone highly esteemed by society — to cor-roborate the product's image.

The Great Admiration: A Malaysian commercial will em-phasize the fame of the brand, assuring the buyer that he or she will share in this fame. Famous brands radiate status.

---

## The Sound of Music

All cultural orientations have a specific tone of voice. The action-oriented British and Americans prefer a positive and promising tone. If an action-oriented manager says your work is "excellent" or "great," he means it is okay. If he uses expressions like "nice" or "quite good," your work was probably insignificant. And listen care-fully to the tone someone uses when they say, "I liked it up to a point." It means you have done a lousy job. Action-oriented cultures also have a strong preference to express developments in terms of growth. Losing money in business is called "negative growth," and a shrinking market is called a "mature" market.

The somewhat process-oriented Germans are more at ease hearing a critical tone of voice than up-beat expressions like "great." To receive positive feedback on their work can be easily perceived as not being taken seriously. They feel they do not need those kinds of comments. ("Who are you to tell me?") More important to them is a clear message about what needs improvement. They are perfectionists. Under achieving is hard to digest. Imagine the "sound" of an American and a German giving each other feedback.

An American's positive "everything is possible" tone of voice has another side effect when dealing with international clients. In their home country, American clients are used to suppliers with a great flexibility in dealing with orders. However, European customers are shocked if a salesperson promises them heaven, but does not live up to it. This occurs quite often when American salespeople travel to Europe to assist the European account managers of their company. By the time these salespeople have returned to the United States, the European account managers have a hard time making up for the harm done by their unfulfilled promises.

## Predictability and Trust

Becoming aware of the differences in cultural styles leads to an easier recognition of the hidden drivers, which leads to a better definition of the problem at hand. With a clear definition, the problem is already halfway solved. The Model of Freedom can help you analyze and define the problem.

I will illustrate this by sharing my experience in a joint venture

---

## Things Can Always Be Improved

Some years ago, while having dinner in Germany with the delegates of a seminar, we learned that the popular German singer Rex Gildo had passed away after having balanced on the brink of death for several days. Gildo had tried to commit suicide by jumping from a third-floor hotel window, drunk. He landed on the lawn.

My German delegates were flabbergasted. The stupidity! Jumping from the third floor! On the grass! If you wanted to kill yourself, you could find a better method than one resulting in several days of suffering.

When I pointed out how German their approach to the incident was, they commented, laughing, *"Es kan ja noch immer besser!"* (Things can always be improved!)

---

between a Dutch company and a German company some years ago.[20] There was trouble brewing between the German and the Dutch departments which were supposed to be merged in the near future. The trust of the German department in its Dutch counterpart had been severely damaged. The Germans complained that they had, time and again, requested complete information on the Dutch department, but to no avail. Sure, they had received partial information, but it was not nearly sufficient to get a complete picture. I found out from the Dutch that they were just as irritated. "These Germans keep insisting on information that has already been sent to them six months ago!"

---

[20]Please keep in mind that the following example involves two companies of more or less equal size. Relationships can be quite different when dealing with two unequal organizations.

In the MoF the Dutch and German dynamic can roughly be presented like this:

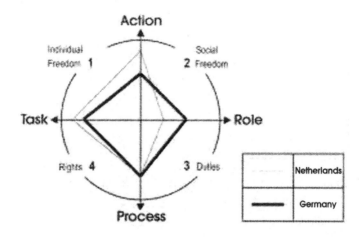

*Sectors 1 and 4, the task-oriented side, largely overlap, so we shouldn't expect many problems in this field. The Dutch and the Germans share the same view on how a task should be fulfilled. In sector 2, however, we notice an important difference between the Dutch and Germans regarding social freedom. A German has more freedom to express his social success, to be a "hero."[21] But that was not an issue in this phase of the joint venture. In sector 3 lies the vital divergence between these two cultures, leading to the problems they were experiencing. This sector represents systems that structure cooperation: information systems concerning control and quality. Germans have a much higher need for those types of structure than the Dutch. This is why the Germans conclude that the Dutch are withholding information, while the Dutch, on the other hand, feel that the Germans are hard to appease.*

---

[21]In modern Germany, "hero" stands for "being socially successful, being a winner," to be celebrated with the purchase of a fine car, for example.

## Extensive e-mails from Portugal

The preference for either content or context also shows between Germanic and Roman languages. I have come across some interesting examples in a lecture by Arie Pos, a professor in literature at the University of Coimbra in Portugal. He demonstrates that Germanic (and Anglo-Saxon) languages will use the phrase "I ran down the stairs," whereas in Portuguese this will be extended to "I descended running down the stairs." Likewise, the English sentence "I ran out of the house," will become "I left the house running" in Portuguese.

Germanic languages only need a verb and a preposition, while Roman languages need a verb to indicate the way in which something was done. And where the Germanic languages are explicit and definite, Roman languages are more general and indefinite.

Once again I borrow an example from Arie Pos. The Portuguese sentence "*Mandei arranjar o carro*" literally means "I have given order to fix my car." But, depending on the context, it can either mean "I had my/the car fixed" or "I have taken my/the car to the service station to be fixed."

No wonder we sometimes hear Northern Europeans and Americans complain about extensive e-mails coming from Portuguese and Brazilian colleagues.

By being aware that a group or person's need for information is culturally determined, we gain clarity and can tackle the real problem. (We will enter into the characteristics of a successful team more profoundly in Chapter 10.)

Building trust is related to predictability of behavior. In a culturally intelligent organization, partners in a joint venture use a cultural marking system to predict how much information their counterpart will need to feel secure and productive. The Germans felt the Dutch were holding out on them, which was very unexpected behavior that led to distrust.

Mind you, we are talking about two cultures that are not even that different. Both appreciate frankness — a difference of opinion will not necessarily lead to paralysis or an escalation of a confrontation. Imagine a task- or action-oriented culture having to build trust with a conflict-avoiding culture like the role-oriented, that limits information or offers information buried in context. It would take a really sensitive cultural radar for a group to catch the right signals, to carefully phrase the right questions to the right person, and then translate the answers to one's own cultural context to give it meaning. People with this kind of cultural intelligence are the elite of the future, even if they are barbarians.

# 7

# Gladiators with Unequal Weapons

*On meetings*

**EmLog Worldwide:**
Jan-Hein van den Brink smells trouble, right from the first agenda item: reviewing the minutes from the previous team meeting. They had been drawn up by Jean-Jacques, since the last gathering took place in Paris. But they contain decisions that apparently had escaped Jan-Hein. Roger and Günther notice this too, and bring it up. But to no avail. Could it be that some team members already got something going last night at the hotel? The three of them had been absent: Roger and Günther took the early morning flight to Amsterdam, and Jan-Hein spent the night at home.

The whole thing reminds Jan-Hein cuttingly of his meetings in Antwerp. In those days his proposals often seemed to be accepted smoothly. He had assumed everyone was on board whenever the Belgians chose not to speak up. Yet none of his plans ever really materialized. With hindsight, he realized that he had underrated the maturity of the decisions of the Belgians. They had merely neglected his input, and that was why his proposed adaptations turned out so futile. The Belgians must have considered him utterly naive.

A conference room can turn into an international arena in which gladiators are combating with trident against sword. The English word "meeting" is one of the most dangerous concepts in intercultural cooperation that I have ever come across. Everyone attributes his own culturally biased meaning to that word. The purpose of a meeting varies according to one's culture. Whenever a variety of cultures is represented in the conference room, misunderstandings, unpleasant surprises, or clear-cut disappointments are likely.

## Styles of Meeting

In an ***action-oriented culture,*** a meeting is an exchange of information with the purpose of coming to some sort of decision. Proposals are sold in an advocating way. Hence we often speak of a *buy-in.* People are enthusiastic to make their case, energized by the challenge of making their targets. A meeting is supposed to conclude with action points. That is a vital detail, even if an action point might be purely semantic, as mundane as "planning a new meeting." Once a decision is made, you do not start pondering on it again. It was with this kind of attitude and cultural reference that EmLog's Rick Delano came to Amsterdam for the kick-off meeting of the project. To him, not getting the buy-in that he had expected was unusual and confusing.

In a ***process-oriented culture,*** people convene to finalize and formalize decisions. The chairman does not appreciate unexpected turns in the discussion during the meeting, even more so if he is the boss. Some preparatory work is required in order to avoid these "whims." A meeting is a kind of ritualized final chord of a decision-making process that has occurred elsewhere, sometimes in secret, but usually not. That is exactly what happened at EmLog. At dinner the night before the meeting, the representatives of the Latin cultures, the Frenchman, the Spaniard, and the Italian, who had to fly in early anyway, had taken the opportunity to probe one another's ideas. It had been a perfect occasion for some preparatory work. The Dutchman, the German, and the Englishman, on the other hand, had judged it more efficient, time-wise, to arrive just before the meeting. Ultimately, they had to pay heavily for their initial efficiency, since they were forced to put in a lot of effort to convince the team to honor some of their preferences.

In a *task-oriented culture,* a meeting is planned to exchange information in order to keep everybody involved in the project. There is a tendency to meet frequently, even when things have already been discussed exhaustively at the coffee corner or around the water cooler. To communicate horizontally in the hierarchy is no problem in a task-oriented culture. Vertical communication, however, is not so easy. Meetings are therefore often the only way for a leader to become informed about the facts and figures, and for subordinates to offer their input. It is important that everybody receives due attention and recognition; otherwise the decision-making process can stagnate. The individual's satisfaction level is important. The Dutchman, Jan-Hein, at EmLog, is a typical representative of a task-oriented culture. During a meeting he needs to feel that there is a consensus, and that everybody feels recognized. He is allergic to political games and pre-cooked decisions. He finds it difficult to get along with colleagues who do not show their cards, or who don't speak up.

In a *role-oriented culture,* a meeting is all about the process, about who gives the input, when, and how. The reason for meeting is secondary; the value is in the ritual of performing it the right way. Surprises and contradictions are discouraged. In many role-

---

### Hon-kaigi, Yobi-kaigi, and Ringi

In Japan, predominantly a role-oriented culture, important meetings are strictly regulated. Everything follows a fixed pattern: who sits where at the table, who can speak first, who can leave the meeting, and who is allowed to drink the first sip of tea. This ritualized meeting is meant to formalize a decision. It is called *hon-kaigi*, the big meeting. A long process of decision-making precedes the meeting; that process usually starts with *nemawashi*, cultivating the field.

More traditional organizations apply *ringi*, a collective decision-making system. Managers fill out specific forms to record their approval, usually sealing them with their personal lacquer stamp. The Japanese make a distinction between *houkoku ringi* for the approval of reports (e.g., the annual report) and *shinsei ringi* for the approval of proposals. *Shinsei ringi* is split up in *houshin, jissi,* and *shusei ringi,* depending on the type of proposal being decided upon.

There also exists a less rigid type of meeting called *yobi-kaigi*, the small meeting. It is a setting in which brainstorming teams try to proceed to the next move. But the ensuing decisions are usually not set in stone.

Yamada from EmLog probably thought he was in a *hon-kaigi* at the kick-off of the project. That is why he came out of the meeting completely confused by all the discussions going on.

---

oriented cultures, silence is the mark of a mature person. A meeting can be perceived as the celebration of a decision. Not everyone is informed on all aspects of the decisions. It's not uncommon for someone to attend a meeting only to discuss one point and then leave when other items are being discussed. This even happens at board level. The decision-making process mostly takes place outside the meeting room or in small sessions beforehand. People with other cultural orientations can find meetings in role-oriented cultures very frustrating.

## Influencing Decisions

In a decision-making process, whether in or outside a meeting, cultural differences can have absolutely unintended consequences. In this respect Timothy Leary's[22] behavioral model is very useful.

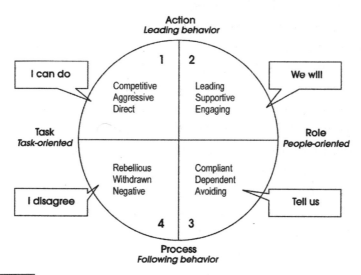

---

[22]The American psychologist and philosopher Timothy Leary (1920–1996) made himself a name in the hippie era with his experiments with drugs. But he also proved to be an outstanding observer and constructed the model known as The Rose of Leary.

Leary noticed that people's spontaneous reactions to others' behavior follow a fixed pattern. I have incorporated Leary's model in my Model of Freedom (see previous diagram) to show how cultures "naturally," as if by reflex, react to each other. It gives insight that enables us to adjust our behavior and communication style in order to effectively influence the behavior of others.

## Spontaneous Reflexes

Leary noticed a "natural" vertical reflex in human behavior. Behavior from sector 1 evokes reflexes from sector 4, and vice versa. Behavior from sector 2 evokes reflexes from sector 3, and vice versa.

Leaders and other "initiators" in task-oriented cultures are often grouped in sector 1. People with another cultural orientation can interpret their behavior as competitive, aggressive, and direct, which can evoke rebellious or withdrawn, behavior. Subordinates in task-oriented cultures and in some process-oriented cultures with a high score on the task-side, like France, are found in sector 4. Their behavior, perceived as rebellious, withdrawn, or negative, often results in a spontaneously competitive and aggressive attitude (sector 1) from people with different cultural orientations.

In sector 2 we find the behavior of predominantly action-oriented cultures. Enthusiastic "we can make it happen" managers easily encourage others to be compliant, timid, or even dependent (sector 3). Many people from role-oriented cultures, like Japan, would feel comfortable in sector 3. Their compliant or dependent attitude toward work encourages others to reflexively "take the lead" (sector 2).

## Taking Your Time

Time has a specific value in every culture. Taking time to think things over can be perceived as a blessing by one culture, but as a curse by another.

In process- and role-oriented cultures time adds to the importance of a decision. The more time spent on a decision, the higher the quality. For representatives of these cultures, quick decisions show that the matter is of a minor importance. They are inclined to interpret the decisiveness of action- and task-oriented cultures as proof of inexperience or immaturity. After all, is it not typical for young people to act without thinking things through? Thus, process- and role-oriented cultures will do everything necessary to stretch the decision-making process, perhaps by involving many people, adding a ceremonial character, organizing a nice dinner, or endlessly discussing all details of a contract. Just think of the election of a new Roman Catholic pope. It takes place in an institute that has without doubt a strong role culture, and the election therefore is a highly ritualized and protracted process that adds to the importance of the decision.

Action- and task-oriented cultures, on the other hand, will make a decision look powerful by coming to a firm conclusion in a short length of time. To accomplish this they may have to simplify issues somewhat, or skip some information just to win time, so they can "get it over with."

## The Golden Rule

Being aware of your own and one another's spontaneous reflexes to a specific cultural attitude is the golden rule in intercultural influencing. By reflecting on the cultural specifics of someone else's attitude, and by recognizing your own culturally biased perception of that attitude, you may find a way to communicate on the same level, thus enhancing the effectiveness of your exchange. If you recognize each other's cultural position, you can avoid being distracted by an apparently aggressive attitude, or become annoyed or impatient with what you interpret as "indecisiveness" or "going against the flow."

Action-oriented people, whose behavior we find represented in the upper half of the circle, can easily find themselves being the initiators, while the rest of the participants act as a passive audience. Both action- and task-oriented people in multinational teams will often have to work with people whose behavior makes them more of a follower than a leader, placing them in the bottom half of the circle.

Role-oriented people, who have an expectant attitude, can be confirmed in their "silence" if other people react by taking the lead and being outspoken.

Process-oriented people often are perceived as too dependent, too subordinate, or too negative, but do not appreciate being "overruled" by initiators. Nevertheless, they provoke such a reaction from other cultural orientations, who automatically react with behavior belonging to the upper half of the circle.

## Conscious Approach

It is possible to actively influence a work situation by taking a conscious approach. In the above model, we can see that it is more effective to choose an attitude that does not belong to the top or bottom sector (vertically), but in a sector alongside (horizontally). For example, if you react supportively (sector 2: "you and me are going to do this together") toward an aggressive attitude (sector 1), you will achieve more than by falling into your spontaneous inclination to be withdrawn or rebellious (sector 4). If you perceive your colleague to be rebellious or withdrawn (sector 4), it will be more effective to put yourself in a dependent or cooperative position (sector 3), than to follow your natural reflexes and clearly express your appreciation (which can be perceived as aggressive, sector 1).

Suppose that your colleague has failed to meet a client's expectations regarding a complaint, and this client keeps calling customer services. You try to get your colleague on the phone, but he does not answer and his voice mailbox is full, too. When you finally reach him, he puts all the blame on this difficult client. Yes, sure, the client has a good point, but what about the enormous workload and staffing problems? This colleague is task-oriented and exhibiting all the behavior from sector 4: he's withdrawn, negative, and accusatory. If you get angry now (sector 1) and read him a task-oriented lecture ("you cannot afford this behavior, this is your responsibility"), chances are that this colleague will get his back up. The discussion will come to a deadlock, and both of you will feel frustrated. However, if you choose to approach him with an attitude from sector 3, for example by explaining that the department's function and your well-being depend on your colleague's behavior while at the same time acknowledging his terrible workload and the like, the colleague will feel called upon to cooperate. But be careful not to come up with the solution yourself. You (being perceived as active) may then very well have to do all the work while your colleague's spontaneous reflex will be to just follow your orders.[23]

---

[23]Of course, all these problems can also arise between people from the same culture. But as has been shown, cultures lean toward one or two of the basic attitudes that we discussed, and therefore encounter these problems more than average.

This warning especially applies to task-oriented cultures, like the Northern European countries, including the Netherlands and Germany. People in these cultures find it terribly difficult to keep their mouths shut when they know how to solve a problem.

## What a Guru Says about Decision Making

For Geert Hofstede, Uncertainty Avoidance is one of the four dimensions on which cultures differ, and also an important aspect of decision making. According to him, the need to avoid uncertainty is what causes decision making to be so time consuming in, for example, Latin cultures.

Hofstede is of the opinion that Anglo-Saxons, who favor decisiveness, are therefore less uncertain than, for example, people in Latin cultures. Our Latin brothers and sisters do not like the sound of that at all. They believe the opposite: people make fast decisions out of uncertainty, to get rid of the pressure of having to make a decision. Fast judgments or instantaneous decisions can reflect a false certainty.

Experience shows that it is a fallacy to assume that process- and role-oriented cultures always work with lingering decision-making processes. On the contrary, people with these orientations are often very flexible, creative, and have a tendency to make last-minute decisions. I believe this reflects a preference for avoiding mistakes, not so much for avoiding uncertainty.

# 8

# Crossing the River Rubicon
## On change processes

**EmLog Worldwide:**
Carlos Vargas faces an issue. The Spanish branch of EmLog has not quite recovered from introducing a new software system about a year ago. The investment is still being felt in the returns, and the employees have not quite adapted — that is, those who have not quit out of sheer discomfort. Carlos can accept that EmLog now wants to work with a uniform system worldwide. But a postponement of at least another year would really help Madrid in terms of the personnel stress level and a write-off of previous investments.

Yesterday Carlos had a conference call with his American team leader and he asked him straightaway how to deal with this. But Rick Delano merely reminded him of the project targets: standardized software for all logistic systems in Europe within a year. That doesn't really help Carlos. "Just go for it" would probably be the best strategy for Emlog Worldwide, but it means that Madrid will have to bleed. Carlos is haunted by a dilemma that he cannot escape without help. He is on the verge of losing courage.

When Julius Caesar and his army stood at the bank of the Rubicon, his decision to cross the river symbolized the start of an enormous change process. Crossing meant declaring war, and there would be no turning back. When it comes to change processes, rivers are a catching image. The Greek philosopher Herakleitos (500 BC) deemed that continuous change was characteristic for every phenomenon: *panta rei,* everything flows. He used the river as a metaphor: it is never the same the next time you step in, because the water runs. Not only has the river changed in the meantime, but so have we, since we have gained new experiences, discoveries, and insights.

Changes in organizations not only need to be managed, they also need to be led. A manager who makes his team cross the Rubicon has to be the leader of his "troops."[24] Strong leadership is a must, because if "everything flows" and the ongoing changes evoke fear, uncertainty and rebelliousness, the manager's authority is no longer self-evident. At EmLog, team leader Rick Delano is risking losing the loyalty of his troops. The Spaniard, Carlos Vargas, expecting leadership in a conflicting situation, is already starting to doubt Rick's competence.

## Threat or Challenge

People respond to change in a variety of ways. To some, change always presents a threat. They feel dislocated or discouraged by the

---

[24]The book *Sunzi Speaks,* based on the more than two thousand-year-old Chinese classic *The Art of War,* is about good leadership in time of war, and explains at length which requirements a good leader should meet. A popular illustrated version is *Sunzi Speaks,* Anchor Books, Doubleday, New York, 1994.

prospect of switching team members, following different procedures and ending up in a new hierarchical or organizational structure. At the other extreme we find people for whom change represents a challenge, a source of inspiration.

People's response to change is in part culturally determined. Some countries have a national culture in which change, and the deriving tension, is accepted or even welcomed. Take the United States,[25] a country with relatively little job security and hence with less income guarantees than most European countries. People easily move from New York to Atlanta, Houston, Chicago, or Washington, if necessary, for a job. Thus, Americans are used to creating a new social environment for their families and to taking initiatives that may again lead to changes.[26] This might explain why the U.S. is the cradle of so many management theories and gurus on change processes. But we often see that an American change theory, put into practice in a country where change is less obvious, meets responses that are not predicted by that theory. There is an analogy in the way American companies operate. For them change is not an issue, neither in their internal processes nor in their external dealings with clients and suppliers. Therefore, they are not at all prepared for the opposition they meet when operating in cultures that are less inclined to welcome change.

---

[25]This example is strictly confined to management aspects. When it comes to "traditional" American values like religion, family, or patriotism, or Americans are not that flexible toward change, as shown by the World Values Survey of Michigan University, see http://wvs.isr.umich.edu/.

[26]This mobility demands smoothly entering into new social contracts and openness toward neighbors and colleagues. Americans often have a positive attitude toward new people and are comfortable with a variety of topics that help get conversations started. As a consequence, they'll often publicly discuss issues that are considered very personal by Europeans.

## Public or Private

Cultures differ in what is seen as appropriate to share with others, what lies in the public domain, and what is meant for a select group of friends and family, the private domain.[27]

The United States differs from other action-oriented cultures by its geography (a vast country) and history (conquering territory, migrating to the West, creating new settlements). If you have to quickly build up a social environment, you need easily accessible information. This is facilitated if you allow a large public domain, which we indeed see reflected in the way Americans behave. When moving into a new home, they invite their neighbors for a barbeque. They rarely feel uncomfortable with someone borrowing their car, and an invitation to stay over is almost never just an empty, polite gesture. Americans welcome you like a friend, but the friendship may end when you have to move.

This large public domain also shows in the floor plan of an American house. In most countries, the front door and living room are separated by a neutral space that works as a filter for people that you do not want to invite in. In the U.S., the front door often leads right into the living room; the heart of the home is public domain. And when Americans move, their furniture is often publicly sold in a garage sale.

---

[27]Already in 1936, Kurt Lewin performed research in this field: "Some social-psychological differences between the US and Germany," *Principles of Topological Psychology*, McGraw-Hill, New York, 1936.

(*cont.*)

In American culture, change is part of people's lives. However, people belonging to a culture with a large private domain, a domain that is carefully built and cherished, will feel a lot more resistance to change. Change is threatening to them, because it affects their private lives, the things they value, that part of life that is supposed to be stable and protected. Process-oriented cultures prefer a large private domain.

## Six Sigma

The implementation of a new software system, like in EmLog, is a change process, as is the implementation of IT systems like Oracle or SAP. When people, rightly or not, feel this as a change toward a system drive with less space for individual freedom, they will react according to their cultural orientation.

Let's examine how each cultural orientation might respond to a major change, using the implementation of Six Sigma in an American company in Europe as an example. Six Sigma is a quality control system that aims to improve efficiency through a strict and simple procedure.[28] Six Sigma ignores the prevailing hierarchy by strategically appointing new team leaders, called green belts and black belts, thus eventually tearing down "empires." Even bolder, Six Sigma builds a parallel organization, a Six Sigma Silo. Implementing this

---

[28]Six Sigma consists of five steps: project definition, measuring, analyzing, testing, and controlling. These steps often involve in-depth analyses and extensive statistical research. Six Sigma is meant to help avoid making mistakes. Therefore, the system has to be strictly obeyed; exceptions cannot be allowed. That is why people who work with Six Sigma feel "system driven."

rigid quality system has a profound effect on an organizational culture and will encounter resistance or encourage "creative solutions" in different cultures.

*Action-oriented cultures* do not show a lot of culture-biased resistance to Six Sigma compared to other cultural orientations, because they use clearly structured processes and measurable data for projects with decisive leaders. Procedures are followed — no exceptions to the rules — but in a pragmatic way, leaving space for individual freedom and responsibility. That pragmatism can sometimes result in conventional projects being afterward conveniently labeled "Six Sigma." If people ever become unmotivated, it is usually caused by the lack of buy-in from representatives of other cultures.

*Task-oriented cultures* may find the incidental irrationality of the Six Sigma application quite a challenge. Occasionally a task is faster accomplished without applying Six Sigma. The Germans, for example, with a less flexible attitude toward systems, will find this a tormenting situation.[29] When Germans strictly follow the prescribed system, which is their preference, they will judge Six Sigma to be a time-consuming and stress-inducing system. Although task-oriented cultures will recognize in Six Sigma a new, common organizational language, chances are that this language won't be appreciated. To Germans, Six Sigma does not support the task because it does not (always) lead to the most efficient way to reach one's goals.

*Process-oriented cultures* have a tendency to see Six Sigma as too simplistic, fearing it may lead to mistakes that will inevitably be discovered by clients. They also fear that they won't get as much done, with consequences for the bottom line, because a system that does not allow exceptions to the rules is sometimes laborious and time consuming. The impression of not working with the right tools

---

[29]German translations of Six Sigma often leave less room for personal interpretation than the original English text, since the German language is more meticulous and rigorous.

causes discomfort and stress. A Spaniard once told me that he looked upon Six Sigma as taking a car to any destination. But you do not go to the second floor by car, do you? Well, Six Sigma said you should! For a process-oriented manager, Six Sigma can be quite frustrating. Anyone trying to implement Six Sigma in a process-oriented culture can expect continuous resistance, and even obstruction.

***Role-oriented cultures*** usually feel quite comfortable with Six Sigma. It is just one of many systems, so a new system and data drive do not pose a problem for these cultures. Six Sigma is generally well managed on account of the inherent need of these cultures to improve systems. For many years, the Japanese have proven to be perfectly at ease with Six Sigma. As we have seen with other originally American systems, for example, the "just in time" system, it is reported to work even better in Japan than in the U.S. There is no danger of de-motivation, because people do not experience any organizational change. Motivation usually is not an issue in role-oriented cultures. Motivation is tantamount to role identification; as long as a person's role is clear, she is guaranteed to be motivated.

## Rewarding Change

*No pain, no change. No gain, no change.* In other words: a change process will only succeed if we agree on its necessity and if our efforts are rewarded. As the Belgian professor and consultant Filip Vandendriessche[30] puts it, "A manager will not get what he wants, but what he rewards."

If we want to successfully manage a change process, we need to reward different cultures in different ways, thereby paying good at-

---

[30]Filip Vandendriessche, *The Input-Output Manager*, Lannoo, Tielt, 1996.

tention to what exactly should be rewarded. Are we sure we're really rewarding those performances that contribute to the desired change?

Again, let's look at a Six Sigma example. In a company with branches in various European countries, some internal suppliers are not cost-effective for that company as a whole due to long production times and large amounts of stock. A company manager decides to apply Six Sigma to cut the prices of the internal suppliers. But it appears that faster production and smaller stock will have a negative effect on the profit of the internal supplier. To complicate this picture, the manager discovers that one of the internal suppliers has previously extended his stocks as a result of a Six Sigma project to bring his manufacturing costs down. This internal supplier will not feel the proposed change process is necessary: *no pain, no change!*

In this example, the optimization of a division's benefits has led to a growing costs development for the company as a whole. Here *input* was rewarded and Six Sigma was applied. Yet, Six Sigma is meant to add to the company's overall turnover. But that *output* is not rewarded in this case, and *no gain, no change!*

In some cultures, a bonus needs not only to be linked to output to be motivating. People lose motivation when their input is not rewarded. Task-oriented cultures frequently reward the effort as well as the result. In 2003, for example, the executive board of Dutch Railways rewarded itself with a bonus for their efforts, although the company's results did not indicate any justification for such a decision. Task-oriented, and occasionally process-oriented, people feel it's necessary to reward good intentions.

## Conflict Management

A change process is most likely to be successful when the people directly involved can maintain their own, culturally determined styles.

Selling a change is like crossing the Rubicon: there is no turning back. The manager or team leader needs total commitment from his or her people. Hence, agreement on the *pain* that causes the need for change is a necessity. This is essential. Of course, differences of opinion on the contents and process of change may lead to heated discussions. But disagreeing on the reason behind a change causes a fundamental problem that can only lead to a schism, resulting in one of the parties leaving the project or company — with or without a bonus.

One does not obtain full commitment through instructions and mapping out a detailed course of action. To a certain extent, everyone involved should feel the freedom to meet their goals in his or her own culturally determined manner, even under the umbrella of one single corporate culture.

Filip Vandendriessche has designed a model for conflict management that, with minor adaptations, can be applied across cultures. In all cultural orientations, with the exception of role-orientation, to offer a solution is asking for trouble, or at least for a lot of discussion. All cultures will find proper arguments to substantiate their disagreement with the proposal of the leader. Instead of coming up with a solution, it is far more effective to start by indicating what criteria should be met and agreeing that the solution that meets these criteria will be accepted. This is not as easy for an expert as it sounds: it's hard knowing the solution and yet keeping your mouth shut![31] When defining the criteria, it is of the utmost importance not to manipulate the team. So, do not be tempted to formulate criteria in such a way that they can only lead to your preferred solution. People are not stupid; they will discover your manipulations and then you will lose their trust.

---

[31] A warning: the Nordic European cultures, in particular, including Germans, will need some exercise in this respect.

In the Model of Freedom, conflict management looks like this:

Task-related conflicts can only arise when there is room for disagreement on the conditions of the execution of the task. In the MoF, on the task side, we can see that if a single solution is offered, counterarguments based on facts and figures will fire back, and an organizational conflict will arise. By offering criteria for a solution, rather than a solution itself, a manager creates commitment in his team. It becomes an individual issue now, and the individual will feel compelled to work on the solution. However, situations may occur in which a team expects the leader to offer a solution and not merely criteria to solve it on their own. In this case, it is preferable to offer more than one solution so your team can become involved in the process of choosing a solution.

By the way, when negotiating the criteria for a solution with your team, the "golden rules" mentioned in the chapters on communication and meetings will prove to be very beneficial.

## Change Is Improving a Copy

Change is often experienced as a threat in role-oriented cultures, like the Chinese and Japanese. For people in these cultures, life is about control, and we all know that change tends to escape complete control. This cultural characteristic is developed in each child from the day he or she learns to write. The Chinese and Japanese languages are written with thousands of pictograms, each drawn with separate strokes. To master a character, you not only need to know its meaning, but also the order and direction in which all the dashes are drawn to form the character. Changes are not allowed, let alone developing your own handwriting. If a young student finds it hard to copy a character correctly, the teacher will lead his hand for a while. Thus, copying has reached the level of an art and has become a way of living. Improvements, often even innovations, are built on existing things. Only the masters, the experts and artists, are allowed to do this.

This has important consequences for the cultural behavior in countries with pictogram writing. Copying is a safe, risk-averse way of working. Instead of changing something completely, they prefer to add existing elements to create something new, analogous to the creation of new characters out of existing ones.

Man + Tree = Rest　人 + 木 = 休
Tree + Tree = Forest　木 + 木 = 林

# 9

# Hunters and Farmers

*On corporate cultures*

**EmLog Worldwide:**

"You Europeans tend to complicate things. All these objections and disputes, what's the use? To me it seems such a waste of time." Akihiro Yamada gets going after a few Heinekens. He and Jan-Hein van den Brink are sitting at the bar of a karaoke place in Amsterdam. Much to Jan-Hein's relief, but to Akihiro's disappointment, the sound system is failing.

Jan-Hein had been complaining about EmLog's inclination toward extreme standardization, throwing doubt on the point of it. Akihiro had no idea what was eating Jan-Hein. "A decision has to be carried out, period. It is not an issue in China or Japan. I truly don't understand why you have to express your own ideas on everything. What is the sense of asking if standardization is needed? The software will be implemented anyway, so why waste your energy and delay the process?"

The seasons impose their steady rhythm to work and social life in rural communities. Plowing, sowing, harvesting, or calving, they all have cyclic patterns to which people have to adjust. The rule in farmers' communities is that property gives power, a power that can take feudal forms. Leaders do not necessarily have to be knowledgeable; their influence is based on property and the degree to which others depend on that. Life in these communities is predictable, bureaucratic, and hierarchical. Insecurity is undesirable, things should be under control, and novelties have to be avoided. Here we find the origin of the "not invented here" syndrome.

Hunters, on the other hand, have to live with uncertainty. Their life is unpredictable and erratic. Times of hard work alternate with times of great leisure, spent in the shade of a tree, where hunters indulge in storytelling, exchanging the interesting details and observations that will help them plan for future successes. A leader should be smart, skillful, and successful. Younger hunters challenge him and compete with him.[32]

Akihiro accepts the intended standardization as something as inescapable as the seasons; Jan-Hein wants to challenge the leader's decisions and would even like to outsmart him.

## National and Organizational Cultures

National or organizational culture is defined by behavior based on a set of values and norms shared with fellow nationals, professionals, or colleagues. National values and norms are not equally important

---

[32]The metaphor of the hunters and farmers derives from D.J. Snowdon, "The Paradox of Story," in *The Journal of Straggly & Scenario Planning*, November 1999.

to everyone,[33] and they are definitely not the only values and norms important to a person. Character, talents, age, intelligence, and other personal characteristics are also quite influential, and they may lead to a specific professional career or a preference for working in a specific type of organization.

When, for example, a person values discipline and feels comfortable within a hierarchy, that person might be well suited for a job in the army or in the police force. These organizations have a role-oriented culture that is irrespective of the national culture. Yet the behavior of a Swedish police officer (whose national culture is task-oriented, with relatively little respect for authority) will differ from the behavior of, for example, a German or French police officer. Cross-border road hogs know all about that. A customer once told me that in Sweden a policeman on a motorcycle who stops you for speeding does not expect you to get out of your car if it is raining cats and dogs. He will address you through the open window, in an admonishing tone. German and French officers, however, are more strongly inclined to discipline and authority, may very well expect you to step out of the car, even if you get your suit wet. Their language will be reprimanding or accusatory. The differences between each officer's behavior derive from their national cultures.

An organizational culture can deviate considerably from the national culture and can carry more similarity to an analogous organization in another country. Take governmental services, such as ministries. Regardless of the country of origin, their organizational cultures have a lot in common.

---

[33]European championship soccer, for example, is well known to be an outlet for large groups to strongly propagate specific national behavior, sometimes quite to the embarrassment of fellow nationals.

## The Salesman and the Lawyer

Some organizations and vocations require a personal cultural orientation that can strongly deviate from the national culture

Regardless of their national culture, good salespersons will have a strong action-orientation. They lure the buyer into making a fast decision, preferably today, and they are going to facilitate this process by emphasizing some strong points of the product, and do not mention information that could delay the decision. Their aim is: just buy it.

On the other hand, good attorneys will be process-oriented, regardless of the national culture they represent. Context is extremely important in this profession, as is looking for exceptions to the rules. And, even if they are part of a national culture that is not very sensitive to authority, attorneys are quite conscious of the fact that, in their profession, it is senseless to challenge the legislative authority.

## Development Stages

An organizational culture changes over time. Not only does it adapt to the outside world (the market, the consumer, the economy), it also has a life cycle. Usually, three stages are distinguished in this cycle, each with its own culture:[34] Start-up, Growth, and Decline (leading to renewal or closing down). It is important to know which

---

[34]For more information see www.legacee.com/FastGrowth/OrgLifeCycle.html, a contribution of Murray Johannsen, chairman of Legacee Inc. My structuring is based on ideas expressed in this article.

stage of the cycle the organization is in, because each stage requires different qualities from its managers, especially Human Resources managers.

In the Start-up stage, an organization needs pioneers and entrepreneurs. In this stage, the organizational culture is usually action-oriented.

In the Growth stage (usually from fast to slow growth) the need for professionals increases. The organization is now strong enough to guarantee career opportunities to professionals, so the organizational culture will slowly change from action-oriented to task- or role-oriented. At the first signs of stagnating growth, the call for "real entrepreneurs" usually increases. Yet, when people with that attitude are indeed recruited, they often encounter strong resistance from the organizational culture because the call for entrepreneurs seems to have been a mere slogan; the true culture in the organization is directed toward perpetuation and risk avoidance.

As soon as an organization finds itself in the Decline stage, and decay is starting to show, the organization becomes introverted and the culture changes into a process-orientation. The organization focuses on its means, not on its goals.[35] Either dramatic changes take place through reorganizations or takeover or people hang on to what they have always done, in the (futile) hope that this attitude nevertheless will lead to improvement. By the time the accountants discover that the organization is in trouble, it is usually too late. If there is no revolution, no cultural shift back to the action-orientation, the end of the organization is near.

Every stage needs people with specific characteristics. It is the responsibility of the Human Resources department to ensure that

---

[35]Take care not to think the reverse. Not every organization with a means- or process-orientation is in decline. Entire industries are, by definition, process-oriented. In the pharmaceutical industry, it can even be dangerous to embrace every day as a new challenge. The crux is in meticulously following instructions and procedures.

those people are available through their recruitment policy and training programs. In the Decline stage, people undergo a culture shock when the organization changes into an action- or task-orientation. People will leave the organization through staff cutbacks or due to the *shake-out* effect. If an organization is in turmoil, people will always start looking for a more suitable working environment. Those who prefer to stay either have a high frustration tolerance and a perfect ability to cope with uncertainty or cannot leave due to personal circumstances like age, mortgage, or specialization. Handling these disillusioned or frustrated employees requires a lot of cultural intelligence from the Human Resources department.

---

### Failed Retention and Return

A Human Resources manager at a Japanese car manufacturer resigned during a period in which many people had to be discharged. The company had come into the Decline stage and was struggling for recovery. The HR manager no longer felt comfortable in a job in which he could not engage in the career planning of employees.

When the company successfully recovered and wanted to attract qualified personnel, this HR manager was again recruited. He returned to his old company. Such a return is almost inconceivable in the Japanese national culture, but it worked very well in the new organizational culture of the company, which was now in a future-oriented stage, matching the professional culture of this Japanese HR manager.

---

## Subcultures

As demonstrated earlier, every organization has its own culture, and so has every stage in the life cycle of that organization. But on top of that, different departments can also have prominent subcultures, like the notorious cultural difference between the manufacturing and the sales department.

Edgar Schein distinguishes three subcultures within an organization.[36] According to him, there is no such thing as *the* Shell culture, for example, and it would be impossible to say that "Microsoft is merciless." He calls the three subcultures Operational, Executive, and Engineering. These three subcultures are mutually conflicting. Representatives of one culture run the risk of misunderstanding representatives of the other cultures.

People who deliver products and services have an Operational Culture. They appreciate teamwork and craftsmanship. Leaders in this culture are people-oriented; financial and technical issues don't matter nearly as much as issues like having the right person in the right place.

In the Executive Culture, we find people who are focused on return on investment: the CEO, CFO, board members, and business unit leaders. They are not primarily driven by loyalty toward employees, but by cash flow and shareholder value. They consider themselves to be lonely heroes, dwelling in a realm above the norms and values of the Operational Culture.

In the Engineering Culture we find engineers and technicians. Their mission is to exclude people from systems. People are considered troublesome tools to be substituted by reliable technology whenever

---

[36]Source: Art Kleiner, "The Cult of Three Cultures," in *Strategy and Business,* 3rd quarter, 2001. Edgar Schein is a professor at the Massachusetts Institute of Technology (MIT). He published the reviewed article in the *Sloan Management Review,* 1996.

possible. Many people have experienced this attitude from, for example, the IT help desk in their organization. When you finally call for their assistance, after a long and lost battle with your computer, they will often tell you there is nothing wrong with your PC, but with you and the way you are handling your computer. No use defending yourself, you have already been labeled a nuisance.

All in all, these three cultures within an organization that look at people entirely differently — as valuable team members (Operational), as replaceable sources (Executive), or as a nuisance (Engineering) — nevertheless must communicate with each other.[37] Looking at an organization in this way, from a cultural perspective (and there are good reasons to do so), it's easy to see that the problems underlying cross-functional teams and operations are actually cross-cultural issues.

## Tension as a Source of Energy

Organizations tend to have a strong preference for one of the four cultural orientations in the Model of Freedom, yet the stage in the life-cycle of the organization and internally diverging preferences (Executive, Operational, and Engineering) are influencing this organizational culture. The organization faces the challenge of turning the tension, generated by these cultural differences, into an advantage. These tensions can be seen as a source of energy for all the nec-

---

[37]This concept of organizational culture has far-reaching consequences for the development of an organization and the role of an organizational development consultant. In particular, the OD consultant may find himself in a difficult situation. How useful is it to advise executives to follow a more "human" approach? Or to let engineers do team-building sessions? Following this path could make them less effective leaders or engineers. (Source: Art Kleiner, ibid.)

essary changes that feed the health of an organization. With their different perceptions, departments keep each other sharp; they are the fuel for the organizational engine. If the action-oriented sales department would fully agree with the process-oriented production department, death would be knocking at the door of this organization. My advice to people who claim that there is no disagreement between those departments of their organization would be to go and find yourself another job. Your company will soon be facing bankruptcy.

Cultural intelligence is what we need to recognize the source of this tension so we don't blame it on bad personal chemistry or incompetence. Not all tensions are healthy for the organization. Irritation caused by miscommunication or manipulation never contributes to the company's turnover. The different perceptions of reality that are represented in cultural differences can be an enrichment that is conducive to alertness, effectiveness, and innovation. The organization's success is not threatened by cultural differences whatsoever, but by lack of trust and by people's uncompromising pursuit of being right. Cultural intelligence does not work if cultural differences are perceived as obstacles that should be cleared, but it does work when we perceive them as obstacles that we can climb in order to have a better view.

## The Confusion between National and Organizational Culture

A Japanese car manufacturer has a production site in the United Kingdom. The production-planning department, which cooperates closely with the sales department, is strongly focused on the market. It is action-oriented. Rapid responses to market demands are a priority, which means

(*cont.*)

that the production-planning department prefers to make a last-minute decision on the number of cars to be produced and their specifications.

The production department, on the other hand, is predominantly process-oriented. It works with complex schedules that can hardly bear sudden changes. This department wants numbers, types, colors, and other specs to be fixed in the earliest possible stage. Preparing a production line to manufacture a car with a different interior or fancy extras may cost a day or more. Planning ahead is the answer to avoiding inefficiencies in the production process.

Whenever the production and production-planning departments meet, two cultures are involved, one process-oriented, the other action-oriented.

If the production-planning manager is Japanese and the production manager is British, the difference in organizational culture is likely to be obscured by the difference in national culture. The Brit does not shy away from arguing in plain terms, in strong pursuit of his preferred solution. The Japanese will most probably show restraint in the face of overt opposition. His answer will be some version of "I understand." We notice here an action-oriented communication style versus a role-oriented communication style.

Cultural intelligence can help you distinguish whether the difference in communication style derives from the national or from the organizational culture. It is vital to see through the differences and focus on a "win-win situation" for the organization. A first step in that direction could involve a decision that is temporarily detrimental for one of the departments, but enhances the success of the company.

## The MoF for Organizations

The MoF distinguishes between doing and thinking, between the visible world of implementations, operations, and actions, and the invisible world of theories, plans and processes. It also proves to be a useful tool for visualizing organizational cultures.

**Action-orientation:** These organizational cultures show a strong focus on the market. They react to a market pull; hence, they work with short-term objectives. They are innovative and dare to take risks. Motivation systems (incentives and rewards) are linked to output and creating heroes. The headcount is flexible and job rotation works in these kinds of organizations. The leader's authority is based on performance; her empowered staff feeds her success. She is decisive. Accountability, job descriptions, and appraisal systems fit into this organizational culture. The organization strives for standardization.

**Process-orientation:** These organizational cultures are focused

107

inward. Operations are based on means and knowledge. They work with middle- to long-term objectives, base their work on substantial research, and avoid risks. They push their products into the market, relying on their technology rather than on market needs. This technology-push creates rather than responds to a need. A strict hierarchy ensures the desired clarity on status, power, and responsibilities. Networking and diplomatic skills are important for advancing one's career and influence. Quality comes before speed. Empowerment, matrix-structures, and "360-degree" feedback systems are unpopular. These organizational cultures do not pursue standardization, but centralization.

*Task-orientation:* Individuals in these organizational cultures relate to each other in a way that is strongly determined by their task. They prefer a flat organization with short communication lines. Hierarchy tends to be ignored as much as possible. Informal communication channels are important, and everyone wants to be informed on many topics, even if they go beyond their work-related interests. These organizational cultures dislike heroism. Leaders are supposed to involve people in the decision-making process. Motivation systems also reward input; dedication and other intangibles can, under the right circumstances, be as highly esteemed as output.

*Role-orientation:* These organizational cultures obtain results through the smooth functioning of teams. They work with middle- to long-term goals. While cooperating, team members will avoid risks and stick to their role in the organization. This attitude favors formality and ritual. Discipline and quality systems perfectly match these organizational cultures. Usually there is no desire for motivation systems or job descriptions. Hierarchy and strong centralization result in absolutely vertical communication. Team members do not exchange information; they may even abstain from social communication. Responsibility for making decisions usually lies with a group. The process of decision making is diffuse or covered by a system that wants the (written) approval of all people involved.

## Organizational Cultures in Central Europe

The assumption that the long history of Soviet rule would have a permanent influence on the cultures in Central European countries has turned out completely wrong. Management styles in countries like the Czech Republic, Slovakia,[38] and Hungary appear to have a lot of similarities, but differ sharply from those in Poland, Croatia, or Romania. Not only do we notice an increased expression of individualism in the Czech Republic, Slovakia, and Hungary, these countries also opt for a strong task-oriented management style. Poland, Croatia, and Romania, on the other hand, often prefer process-oriented management styles.

This may very well indicate that the Central European countries are returning to their pre-communist cultural preferences, from a role-oriented culture (that fits the planned economy of the communist system) back to a task- or process-oriented culture. Remnants of the communist era can be found — a company led by a former member of the communist party or old authorities clinging to power and keeping an informal influence through their firm network left over from communist times — but they are almost extinct.

---

[38]I published research paper on Slovak management styles in November 2002. "Accenture Bratislava: The Slovak Management Style," see www.cmc-net.org/publications.

# 10

# Ceci n'est pas un team

*On a winning intercultural team*

**W**hat makes an intercultural team a winning team? Rick Delano and his team were facing quite a challenge, an assignment containing a lot of complicating elements. But with all that talent on the team, success should have been easy. The fact that it wasn't means that you need more than expertise to succeed; you need cultural intelligence.

## A Team Is a Living Paradox

Every team is a living paradox.[39] An example of paradoxical information is when Delano says, "Bauduin is a liar" and Bauduin re-

---

[39]K. Smith and D. Berg, "Cross-Cultural Groups at Work," *European Management Journal*, February 1997.

sponds with "Delano tells the truth" Looking at this concept from a team perspective, the individual is essential for the quality of a team, but a person has to give up some of his individuality to enhance the quality of a team. Because of this paradoxical situation both the individual and the team are confronted with a dilemma.

Earlier in this book, we found that the cultural identity of a person stems from an ongoing process of reconciling the dilemma between individuality and role behavior. The same goes for teams, but at a higher, more complex level, since more persons are involved. The cultural identity of a team is an ongoing process of reconciling the dilemma between the individual's input and the team's performance. Winning teams do not try to solve this dilemma by choosing for either the team or the individual, nor do they compromise between the two. On the contrary, they empower individuality through teamwork, and enhance teamwork through individual contributions. It is not one or the other, but attaining one through the other.

Everyone is familiar with the negative version of team behavior as embodied by a gang hassling passers-by. The members of the gang share responsibility for individual acts, which gives the individual a feeling of security and power. A single boy in this gang will dare to act in a way that he would not dream of doing if he were alone. Both he and his "team" share the power generated by his acts and eventually they will also share the catch.

The positive version of a winning team resembles its negative, but it takes place within the boundaries of ethics and law, and often with a more complex aim.

## Team Cultures

The way people reconcile the dilemma and build a winning team depends on their cultural orientation. Each cultural orientation has its own preferred team culture, which has consequences for the relationship between the individual and the team.

*Action-orientation:* A team is conceived as a group of people working together to achieve a goal that an individual alone could not achieve. Individual contribution and responsibility mark the standard of quality in this team. Admiration is not directed toward team accomplishments, but toward the exceling individual, sometimes the lonesome cowboy. In these cultures team building is integrated in educational programs, because qualities like cooperating and sharing are not obvious. Team members relate to each other as long as the team needs to achieve its goal. After that the team disintegrates. A team is successful if the individual can identify with the success of the team, if it feels like his or her success.

*Process-orientation:* A team is conceived as a group of people who relate to each other through a complex constellation of rights, duties, obligations, rituals, and hierarchy. These teams are sharp and fast under strong leadership, but without it they tend to favor risk avoidance and a lack of individual initiatives, not because of incompetence, but because members feel they are held responsible for things beyond their scope, or because they feel "unprotected." That is why these teams have trouble working in matrix structures in which it is not always crystal clear who is in charge of what. Often they will see the functional boss as the one in charge, not the team leader. A team is successful under strong leadership if it leaves sufficient space for individual interpretations.

*Task-orientation:* Like in action-oriented cultures, a team is conceived as a group of people working together to achieve a goal that could not have been achieved by one single person. The main difference is that lonesome cowboys and other heroes are not particularly appreciated. Basic principle is that all team members are equal. Since the individual does not benefit from exceling — the group might even accuse him or her of showing off — motivation is found in team performance, in encouraging the feeling of "we." The individual has a tendency to emphasize his rights at the expense of his duties, as he needs to emphasize his individuality to balance the "we." A team is successful if all members feel involved in all decisions.

*Role-orientation:* In these cultures, the individual is subordinate to the team. A high level of internal discipline and strong team roles characterize these teams. The different roles of the team members bind them, because they are complimentary. Lonesome cowboys are taboo; responsibilities and honor are shared. The individual often strongly identifies with the team. Although a task provides structure and defines relationships, the team spirit will not completely disappear after the team is dissolved. A functional relationship may continue to last over years, even if members have since joined other teams. This sometimes grows into a strong network. A team is successful if the individual has the feeling that he or she is able to fulfill his or her duties to the team.

## Characteristics of an Effective Team

Before jumping to the characteristics that make an intercultural team a winning team, we will first take a closer look at what makes a monocultural team tick.

What makes a monocultural team successful?

1. The team members agree on the common goal.

2. They agree on the strategy.

3. They agree on the structure of the team.

4. They know each other's team roles.

5. They exchange information.

As a consequence of these five characteristics, we see a team culture develop. After all, if everything goes by the book, we start with developing a strategy aimed at achieving our goals. Only then, in line with the strategy, do we feel the need for structure in the team. Based on that structure, people will relate to each other in a specific way, and thus will create a culture. If people then exchange information they will become predictable for each other. This predictability prevents the occurrence of surprises, and gradually we build trust and commitment. A we-feeling has developed; we start speaking of "our team" and "us."

When a bank once invited me for a team building session at director's level, I could not get a clear reply to my question: what is your common goal? To me this meant that this team degraded into a group of people working together with the best intentions, but without the added value of being a team. The added value is precisely this commitment to a common goal, and not just commitment to your interpretation of the common goal.

If building a monocultural team already is this difficult, one can imagine the effort it takes to get a multicultural team to function well. Each of the four cultural orientations has its own interpretation of the characteristics of effective teams. It is vital that we make these interpretations explicit. What do we mean by "common goal"? What strategy do we apply, and why? Are we clear about the structure of the team, the hierarchy, and the responsibility attached to certain team roles? Crucial for the success of the intercultural team, however, is the exchange of information, since that lays the foundation for trust building and we-feeling.

## Trust, the Cement between Cultures

As demonstrated in previous chapters, culture profoundly affects the type of information people share, the amount of information exchanged, as well as the preference for certain information channels. Cultural differences may lead to miscommunication or, worse, distrust. Modern communication techniques, such as e-mail or videoconferences, will sooner obstruct than create the building of confidence, but there is no way going without them. Information exchange, no matter how, is important for building trust between team members.

We distinguish three types of trust important to a business situation:[40]

1. Contractual trust: trust based on reciprocal self-interest

2. Rational trust: knowledge-based trust

3. Emotional trust: identification-based trust

In a case of contractual trust, parties will trust each other as long as the advantages of not breaking an agreement outclass the disadvantages. That is why normally contracts are broken if the benefits are higher than the fine. I will not elaborate on contractual trust, as it mostly occurs between strangers and therefore is not relevant to teamwork.

Rational trust is based on the extensive predictability of each other's behavior, achieved through knowledge and experience: "I know she will act like this in that situation, since I've seen it before and I understand her reasons."

Emotional trust, however, is a matter of feeling a bond not founded on a rational explanation for someone's behavior: "I trust him, because he is the friend of my best friend."

---

[40]Based on D.L. Shapiro, B.H. Sheppard, and L. Cheraskin, "Business on a Handshake," *Negotiation Journal,* 1992, pages 365–377.

## Rational and Emotional Trust

Cultural intelligence is key to building rational and emotional trust because it helps to recognize what drives people.

Rational trust is fed through information, but that also has its pitfalls, as the significance of information is different in all cultural orientations. People from action- or task-oriented cultures score low on the scale of how much information they need, compared to people from process- and role-oriented cultures. We also discovered important differences in the kind of information that is expected and the way it is communicated. In the process of information exchange, all parties may have the impression that they did not get what they asked for (too little, too much, not relevant). This causes little understanding for each other's drives and motives, which is not favorable for the predictability of each other's behavior. It is therefore of the utmost importance for intercultural teams to clarify their information needs and to learn to listen closely to unusual inquiries and requests for information. Cultural intelligence, in this case, means being able to imagine the information needs of another person.

Emotional trust, the *feeling* that you can trust another, even when they display unexpected behavior, is a kind of we-feeling. That we-feeling is not impaired by incidental failures, thanks to a strong feeling of solidarity. Team members can reach the level of emotional trust via rational trust, but emotional trust can also be that "click," that unshakable and spontaneous feeling of "we fit together." Emotional trust arises if people share values. Cultural intelligence helps to uncover those values and to transform them into norms.

It is a kind of trust that one cannot achieve through e-mail. It may be maintained by e-mail, but it will more likely be smashed. The same is true for conference calls and videoconferences. These techniques do not have the same impact as being physically present, in the same room. Identification, that is, emotional trust, does not easily arise from electronic communication media. Unconsciously, we are always looking for signals that inform us about the trustworthiness of a person. If the circumstances are not optimal, we become alert, and even a minor incident can be alarming, feeding distrust. Starting off a virtual team therefore always means convening a confidence-building session. Skipping this phase results in people cooperating from a distance, for better or for worse, but without ever achieving teamwork.

*This Figure illustrates how the Model of Freedom works with trust.*

## The Culturally Intelligent Team

An intercultural team is an amalgam of different team roles, information needs, and convictions about the truth. Every participant should be aware of this. That is not quite obvious for action-oriented people, who tend to think "If it is not tangible, it does not exist." Task-oriented people may find it difficult to cope with the apparent inefficiency of role-oriented team members: "Skip the procedures, let's not lose time." Role-oriented people, for their part, interpret the apparent lack of discipline in task-oriented people as a sign of incompetence: "Don't ask why, ask how." Process-oriented people may find it difficult to picture everybody's responsibilities and therefore opt for a "creative solution": "What you propose seems to be impossible" might be the first impression of a creative solution.

What is the panacea for a winning intercultural team?

Awareness is a first and important step. The moment we realize that culture is at stake, we can use the MoF to map the differences in information needs. After having pinned down all the differences — identifiable in the non-overlapping parts in the diagrams in the MoF — the team can work out the best ways of coping with them. From this point on, the team will enter a process of confidence building. The conditions for teamwork are created.

Next step is the distribution of team roles. What at first sight appears as a mess of deviating perceptions of team roles now has to be turned into an advantageous situation in added value, synergy. Each team member should get a culturally fitting team role. Without this sensitive approach to the national, organizational, department or vocational cultures present, we may end up with unworkable situations. Imagine "an initiator" being assigned to prepare non-standardized data-analyses, on which "an analyst" has to found his decisions. This "analyst" will most probably judge the data insufficient for a decision, whereas the "initiator" feels frustrated because he does not expect to see any action coming from this team. It is much more effective to hand over all data-analyses to process-oriented people, and leave all short-term objectives and fast decisions to action-oriented people. In such a design an intercultural team will out-perform mono-cultural teams. The "weak spots" of one cultural orientation are counter-balanced by the "strong spots" of another cultural orientation. Protracted decision-making processes and risk avoiding moves will be compensated with decisiveness and actions. If things go too fast, and decisions risk being based on insufficient data, the call for reflection from process-oriented people will be very beneficial for the team. Likewise, the individualistic attitude of task-oriented team members will not necessarily lead to delays thanks to the discipline of the role-oriented team members.

It may be superfluous, but I want to stipulate once more a very important condition: nothing works without the recognition of and the respect for each other's cultural orientation. In addition, we should keep in mind that we are never working toward a compromise, a situation in which all parties feel they had to give in, but we are working toward reconciliation.

## Best Practices

In the MoF we juxtaposed Action versus Process and Task versus Role. A compromise between Action and Process delivers delayed actions and interrupted developments. A compromise between Task and Role delivers undisciplined team members who try to escape their responsibilities.

A culturally intelligent team utilizes the tensions between the extremes as a source of energy, and as a drive to incorporate the best of the four cultural orientations, so the whole will become more than the sum of the parts.

This asks for leadership. Rick Delano, the American team leader at EmLog, has what it takes to be a leader, and from a cultural point of view he is the right man in the right place. But, as a leader, he should not only exploit his action-orientation, emphasizing targets as such. He better come up with a larger repertoire in how to meet targets. He can deploy his charisma in a way recognizable to the Latin Europeans, even if it means flying to Paris with no other aim than giving status to his local subordinates. And, although it is not his preferred way of delegating, it is not impossible for him to give assignments that are more closely related to the intended actions. And how about communicating his expectations more clearly? He could, for instance, have given the German Günther specifics on going deep, but not that broad. Certainly he can prevent the Dutchman Jan-Hein from withdrawing from the group, for example by letting him feel that his input is needed for the collaborative effort of the team.

All these examples of actions might seem to be completely redundant, and so they may be for action-oriented people. Nevertheless, people from all cultures can undertake these actions, simply by abstaining from holding on to their "being right," and focusing on desired effects.

If we succeed, not only in building our team with cultural intelligence, but also in applying all of the cross-cultural skills discussed in this book, our team will no doubt become a champion in the international arena.

# Appendix I

## The Theories of Hofstede and Trompenaars

*The scholars Geert Hofstede and Fons Trompenaars both pioneered in cross-cultural studies. They achieved guru status in the field of organizational development and more generally in social sciences. I will summarize their well-known models and concepts.*

### Geert Hofstede

Hofstede has had a profound influence on the development of cultural studies in social science, since his publication of *Culture's Consequences* in 1980. His research (1968 and 1972) is based on 116,000 questionnaires within the IBM company. Hofstede designed a model with four dimensions to give meaning to his findings. He later added a fifth dimension, Chinese Work Dynamism, based on parts of the work of M.H. Bond,[41] who independently performed research among Chinese students. Recently Hofstede added several countries to his research list, again based on research outside of

---

[41]M.H. Bond, *The Rokeach and Chinese Value Surveys*, 1988.

IBM. I confine myself to his original IBM research, still used by Hofstede and his school.

Hofstede defines four dimensions in which he demonstrates how national cultures differ. He found these dimensions through theoretical reasoning and statistical analyses.[42] He assumes that culture does not change, or, since he did find some deviations between the first and second stages of his research, that cultures all change in the same way, so that this change does not affect the significance of the scores on the questionnaire. He has not been able to scientifically verify this assumption since he did not get the chance to repeat and validate his research at IBM.

Hofstede's dimensions are:

**Power Distance** (from low to high)
The extent to which people accept the unequal distribution of power in a society.

**Individualism** (from collectivism to individualism)
The extent to which people are integrated in groups. The scale starts with people who feel they belong to groups, and who think in terms of "we." On the other end of the scale, we find people who only look after themselves and their immediate family, and who think in terms of "I."

**Masculinity** (from feminine to masculine)
A caring (feminine) community, focused on quality of life issues, versus a competitive and harsh (masculine) community. This can be measured in the differences in social roles between men and women.

**Uncertainty Avoidance** (from low to high)
The extent to which people feel threatened by uncertainty and try to avoid these situations; also the extent of tolerance toward the unknown.

---

[42]*Culture's Consequences*, Abridged edition, Geert Hofstede, Sage Publications, London, 1984, page 11.

## Fons Trompenaars

Trompenaars received his Ph.D. for a comparative study on concepts of organizational structure in different cultures.[43] Trompenaars chose existing dimensions to classify his cultures, and found them at the famous researchers C. Kluckhohn and F.L. Strodtbeck.[44] Five of his seven dimensions are related to human relations, the other two describe the relation of humans to time and nature. The total number of questionnaires used until today in Trompenaars' research is approximately 50,000. Trompenaars assumes that cultures change, and he updates his country scores regularly. The questionnaires cover a wide range of organizations and countries.

Trompenaars' dimensions are:

## Universalism versus Particularism

Seeing rules as universally applicable, to be strictly followed, versus applying rules depending on the context (like favoring friends or family).

## Individualism versus Communitarianism (Collectivism)

Taking full responsibility for one's own actions, thinking in terms of "I," versus sharing responsibilities with a group and thinking in terms of "we." (The only dimension to be found in both Trompenaars' and Hofstede's model.)

## Specific Orientation versus Diffuse Orientation

A differentiating attitude (look at facts and events separately, non-related), versus a holistic, "everything is related to everything" attitude.

---

[43] "The Organization of Meaning and the Meaning of Organization," The Wharton School of the University of Pennsylvania, 1983.
[44] Ibid, page 60.

## Neutral Orientation versus Affective Orientation

Reluctance to show emotions versus freely expressed emotions.

## Achievement Orientation versus Ascription Orientation

Status based on performance versus status attributed by virtue of age, gender, ancestry, and so forth.

## Time Orientation

The relative importance cultures give to the past, the present, and the future, and their preference to structure time as a sequential process (planning and executing one thing after the other) or synchronic processes (working in different "time-tracks" simultaneously).

## Nature

Dominating over nature, versus submission to nature.

## The Differences Between Hofstede and Trompenaars

From the public discussion between Hofstede and Trompenaars regarding their differing views I concluded that the source of their disagreement can be found in their different professional cultures.[45]

Hofstede shows a strong process-orientation. He built a complex theory, striving for perfection, partly by pure thinking and reasoning, that explains the real, physical world of cultures the way it was manifest in his research. When reality does not seem to match the theory in the eyes of others, Hofstede argues that people have either misunderstood the theory or a peculiar view on reality.

---

[45]Discussion in *International Journal for Intercultural Relations*, vol. 20, no. 2, 1996 and vol. 21 nos. 1 and 2, 1997.

Trompenaars, on the other hand, shows a strong action-orientation, maybe partly influenced by the fact that he did his research in the United States. He masters the language of action-oriented cultures, and is very successful in these countries. Trompenaars uses expressions like, "When it works in reality, the underlying theory must be all right."[46] This statement shows that Trompenaars is concentrating on reality (of managers), and is willing to adjust his theory if it does not work in reality.

It is an interesting confrontation between the scientist Hofstede, austerely trying to unveil what is false or true, and Trompenaars, a talented communicator who wants to educate people in the awareness of cultural differences, and has created a very effective learning process.

We recognize in them the process-oriented person — "prove it to me" — versus the action-oriented person — "show it to me." In the MoF I am directed toward the reconciliation of these two cultural orientations. The MoF is neither a compromise nor the expression of a preference for one or the other.

---

[46]Statement noted during Trompenaars' presentations, when the author worked with Trompenaars in different locations confirmed on inquiry by the author.

# Appendix 2

## The Origins of the Model of Freedom

### Introduction

It is a longstanding tradition in social sciences to criticize the research and methodologies of fellow researchers. Certainly, Hofstede and Trompenaars have had their fair share of criticism. In my opinion, criticism is a good habit among scientists, and it serves scientific progress, as long as the criticism is not ad hominem. However, I do not intend to evaluate the scientific caliber of the research performed by these two "culture pioneers." I fully recognize the value of their work that has proven to be very important to developing my Model of Freedom.

### Research Method and Scores

When working with Hofstede's and Trompenaars' models in the past, I interviewed international managers on what they experienced as instructive and, of course, the discussion also turned to what they considered to be its weaknesses. For these interviews I did not use questionnaires, but applied the "Appreciative Inquiry" as a method. This method addresses what works well, instead of focusing on problematic situations. People feel invited to give realistic answers, based on experience, and not on what is esteemed to be socially or politically correct; not the "I would have," but "I did."

To determine a score on a dimension in my model, I have operated as follows. Let's take the dimension "Individuality." When training an international group of managers, I showed a score of Trompenaars (or Hofstede, depending on the preference of the client for either one of these models at that time), and I illustrated the consequences for the management style. In the subsequent discussion with managers from different nationalities, they would decide if the country score would be recognized as valid or not. If not, we discussed what, according to their experiences, they thought the correct score should be. After a number of these exercises, I took the average score as an indication. It is not scientifically founded, and I immediately admit that, but it does result in scores that mirror the practice of people currently working in the international arena.

In the past twelve years, I have assembled the repeated and persuasive feedback of some 5,000 internationally operating managers, which led to adjustments in the scores of both Hofstede and Trompenaars. As this goes entirely against Hofstede's idea that culture does not change, it finally led us to go our separate ways.[47]

The country diagrams in my database, numbering forty-eight at the moment,[48] have derived from this method. I do not pretend to

---

[47]In my opinion, cultures do definitely change. You cannot neglect the effects of globalization, leading to similar consumer behavior in such differing countries as China and Nicaragua, of Islamization, changing the habits of millions of people in a country like Indonesia, of economic unity in the European Union, a process that affects such differing countries as Lithuania and Ireland. But although cultures change, the cultural orientation remains quite steady. The membership of the EU has not changed the action-orientation of the British or the process-orientation of the French.

[48]I did not show all forty-eight diagrams of my database, because every diagram needs an explanation. I confined myself to present the diagrams that clearly represent the four cultural orientations. To use the MoF effectively it is not necessary to have all the forty-eight diagrams in mind.

do anything more than giving an indication of cultural preferences. I have not been looking for exact percentages. My belief in the practical value of accurate numbers in this field has decreased immensely during my career as a trainer.

## The Dimensions

Not only have the scores been adjusted in the course of the years, so have the dimensions. As a result the MoF shows a reconciliation of Hofstede's and Trompenaars' approaches, thus enhancing its analytical and didactical value.

## Authority

The dimension of "Authority" is absent in Trompenaars' model. Hofstede has the dimension "Power Distance," but only related to "ascribed status," even though he does not mention that explicitly. "Achieved Status" shows up in Hofstede's model in "Masculinity," a dimension that I do not use because it has no explanatory value in the MoF. I link "Authority" to responsibility and differentiate between ascribed status and achieved status as a source of authority, based on Trompenaars' status definitions.

## Systems

The dimension "Systems" stands for the cultural need for simple or complex rule systems. The similarity with Hofstede's dimension "Uncertainty Avoidance" is deceptive. I am convinced that the need for simple or complex systems is just a different expression of dealing with the same feeling of uncertainty. The connection with Trompenaars' "Universalism" (simple system) and "Particularism" (complex system with exceptions to the rules integrated into the system) is evident. Universalists deal with uncertainty by making a clear universal choice (and thus avoid uncertainty). Trompenaars' particularists, on the other hand, believe that taking the context of every decision into account is the best way to avoid the uncertainty of possible mistakes. Then one feels the tension drop when having made the decision to "just do it." The other is relieved after feeling sure about the decision, based on ample consideration.

## Individualism

The dimension "Individualism" does have some similarities with Hofstede's and Trompenaars' dimension, but there is a fundamental difference. I do not define "Individualism" as the opposite of "Collectivism." One can be an articulated individualist, but at the same time have a high score on some aspects of collectivism. In the United Kingdom and the United States, where individuals have many rights, people also tend to conform to their class or community (an aspect of collectivism), and show great discipline (a virtue based on not giving priority to your individual preferences). So, within the same culture, one can have a high score on Individualism and on Collectivism, the dimension "Role Behavior" in the MoF.

## Role Behavior

This dimension measures the extent of an individual's identification with his or her social role or team role. Together with "Individualism," it constitutes the cultural identity of a person. In a community people always think in terms of "I" and "we," depending on the situation. This cannot be expressed in a culture model if "Role Behavior" is characterized as a low score on "Individuality." That is why "Role Behavior" is an independent dimension in the MoF.

Based on these four dimensions, four cultural orientations can be discerned in the MoF: *Action, Process, Task,* and *Role.*

## Construction Elements of the MoF

To assemble my MoF, I have naturally studied other organizational culture models and behavioral models, apart from Hofstede and Trompenaars. Edgar H. Schein, Robert E. Quinn and Kim S. Cameron, Roger Harrison and Herb Stokes, David A. Kolb and Timothy Leary particularly inspired me.

The way I have constructed the MoF shows both action-oriented and process-oriented elements. The action-orientation proves itself in my approach of learning from reality and pragmatically adjusting the theory. On the other hand, a process-orientation is discernable in acquiring knowledge through the work of many scholars, applying them, testing them, thinking them through, and finally, distilling new dimensions.

The didactic value of my model surfaces in the visualization of cultural differences through diagrams. I am not interested in the mathematical accuracy of that diagram. What I am after is that people recognize their culture in a diagram and learn from the comparison with the diagrams of other cultures. In this respect, my MoF has proven to be very effective.

# Appendix 3

## The Model of Freedom in One View

All national and organizational cultures fit into four cultural orientations.

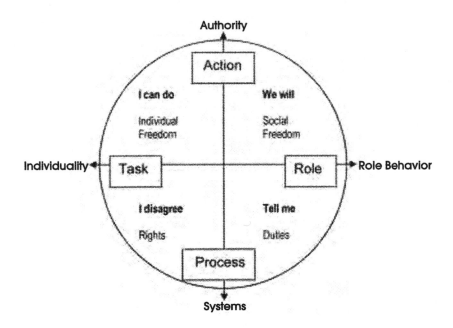

Definitions

*Culture:* A set of shared norms and values of a group expressed in the behavior of the group members.

*Cultural Identity:* The two components of Cultural Identity are Individuality and Role behavior.

*Cultural Behavior:* The expression of our cultural identity. Our behavior is limited by Authority and guided by Systems (rules) corresponding to our culture.

*Authority:* The authority of a leader is based on achieved or ascribed status.

*Achieved* status: The respect you earn from others based upon what you do.

*Ascribed* status: The respect you earn from others based upon who you are.

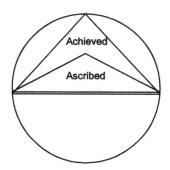

*Systems:* Cultures use either simple or complex systems to protect and control the individual and the community.

*Simple systems:* Systems that allow no exception to the rule.

*Complex systems:* Systems in which rules are context dependent.

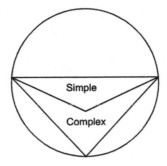

*Individual behavior:* Characterized by a belief in personal responsibility for your actions; the right to speak up, to disagree with peers, and to challenge authority; strong task orientation; do it your way, be different; use direct communication.

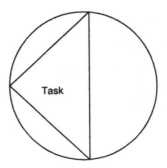

***Role behavior:*** Characterized by a belief that the community dictates your behavior; discipline, shared responsibility and conflict aversion are valued; relationships are important to achieve a task; indirect communication.

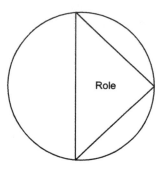

## Action-orientation

Just do it. Get started. I don't care how you do it. Keep it simple. Be decisive. You have to be a winner. Make things visible. Be positive. Everything is possible.

## Process-orientation

Always be well prepared. Have intelligent arguments at hand. Hierarchy is imported and should be respected. Decisions may take time. Life is a complex process. *Savoir vivre.*

## Task-orientation

We work together because we have a common task. Be direct and content driven. Personal accountability. Need to feel involved. Individual responsibility. Be critical if needed.

## Role-orientation

Everybody has his role and obligations. Task is the result of a team effort. We share responsibility. Most communication is vertical and indirect. Focus on relations. Don't confront people.

# Appendix 4

## Train the Trainers

It is common practice in the world of trainers and consultants to learn from each other. And why would anyone oppose that? As long as the content of this work is recognized as my intellectual property and the copyrights are not violated, I am happy to contribute to this community.

I am, however, concerned about the brand image of the Model of Freedom. The MoF has a high potential and has more applications than can be disclosed in a book. In the book I gave a demo-version of the MoF. A critical and experienced audience can easily corner a trainer who does not have a full grip of the MoF. My worries are that incapable trainers might cause damage to the reputation of the MoF.

In order to prevent this, I conduct master classes for trainers, consultants, and human resources managers with an international track record of at least five years. In these master classes, I train them to use the MoF at its full potential in their specific professional fields.

Information on these Train the Trainers classes can be found on the CMC website: www.cmc-net.org.

# Appendix 5

## Literature

Bayne, Rowan, *The Meyers-Briggs Type Indicator*, Chapman & Hall, London, 1995.

Dessler, Gary, *Organization Theory — Integrating Structure and Behavior*, Prentice-Hall International Editions, London, 1986.

Elliott, Charles, *Locating the Energy for Change: An Introduction to Appreciative Inquiry*, IISD, Winnipeg, Canada, 1999.

Fennema, Elbrich, *Hoe Japan Werkt*, Atlas, Amsterdam/Antwerp, 1996.

Feyerabend, Paul, *Against Method*, Verso, London, 1978.

Francesco, Anne Marie, and Barry Allen Gold, *International Organizational Behavior — Text, Readings, Cases and Skills*, Prentice Hall, London, 1998.

Funakawa, Atsushi, *Transcultural Management*, Jossey-Bass, San Francisco, 1997.

Goleman, Daniel, *Emotional Intelligence*, Bloomsbury, London, 1996.

Hall, Edward T., *The Silent Language*, Doubleday, New York, 1959.

Hampden-Turner, Charles (with Fons Trompenaars), *The Seven Cultures of Capitalism*, Doubleday, New York, 1993.

Harris, Philip R., and Robert T. Moran, *Managing Cultural Differences*, 3rd edition, Gulf Publishing Company, London, 1991.

Hendon, Donald W., and Rebecca Angeles Hendon, *How to Negotiate Worldwide*, Gower, Aldershot, UK, 1989.

Hofstede, Geert, *Culture's Consequences*, Sage Publications, London, 1984.

——, *Interkulturelle Zusammenarbeit — Kulturen, Organizationen, Management*, Gabler, Weisbaden, 1993.

——, *Masculinity and Femininity — the taboo dimension of national cultures*, Sage Publications, London, 1998.

——, *Cultures and Organizations, Software of the Mind*, McGraw-Hill, 1991.

——, *Exploring Culture*, (with Gert Jan Hofstede and Paul B. Pederson), Intercultural Press, Yarmouth, ME, 2002.

——, "Riding the Waves of Commerce," in *The International Journal of Intercultural Relations*, vol. 20, 1996.

——, "Riding the Waves, a rejoinder," in *The International Journal of Intercultural Relations*, vol. 21, 1997.

Imai, Masaaki, *Kaizen — the Key to Japan's Competitive Success*, Random House Business Division, New York, 1986.

Kleiner, Art, "The Cult of Three Cultures," in *Strategy and Business*, 3rd quarter, 2001.

Kolb, David A., *Experience as the Source of Learning and Development*, Prentice Hall, London, 1985.

Leary, Timothy, *Interpersonal Diagnosis of Personality — A Functional Theory and Methodology for Personality Evaluation*, Ronald Press Company, New York, 1957.

Lévi-Strauss, Claude, *The Savage Mind*, The University of Chicago Press, Chicago, 1973.

Lewin, Kurt, *Principles of Topological Psychology*, McGraw-Hill, New York, 1936.

Machiavelli, Nicolo, *The Prince*, translated by W.K. Marriott, eBooks@ Adelaide, 2004.

Mastenbroek, W.F.G., *Conflicthantering en Organisatieontwikkeling*, 3rd edition, Samsom BedrijfsInformatie, Alphen aan den Rijn, 1992.

Paul, J.C.L., M.R. van Gils, L. Karsten, M.A.G. van Offenbeek, and J. de Vries, *Organisatie en Gedrag*, Kluwer Bedrijfswetenschappen, Deventer, 1994.

Quinn, Robert E., and Kim S. Cameron, *Diagnosing and Changing Organizational Culture*, Addison-Wesley, New York, 1999.

"Salary Man" in Japan, Japan Travel Bureau, 1991.

Sanders, Geert, and Bram Neuijen, *Bedrijfscultuur: Diagnose èn Beïnvloeding*, Van Gorcum/Stichting Management Studies, 4th edition, Assen, 1992.

Shapiro, D.L., B.H. Sheppard, and L. Cheraskin, "Business on a Handshake," in *Negotiation Journal*, 1992.

Schein, Edgar H., "Three Cultures of Management: The Key to Organizational Learning," *Sloan Management Review*, 38, 1, 1996.

—— *Organizational Culture and Leadership*, Jossey-Bass Publishers, London, 1987.

Smith, K. and D. Berg, "Cross-Cultural Groups at Work," *European Management Journal*, February 1997.

Smith, Peter B., "Culture's Consequences: Something Old and Something New," in *Human Relations*, vol. 55, 2002.

Snowdon, D.J., "The Paradox of Story," in *The Journal of Straggly & Scenario Planning*, November 1999.

Sun Tzu, *The Art of War*, Dover Publications, New York, 2002.

Tannen, Deborah, *Talking from 9 to 5*, Dutch edition, Prometheus, Amsterdam, 1994.

Trompenaars, Fons, "The Organization of Meaning and the Meaning of Organization," The Wharton School of the University of Pennsylvania, 1983.

——(with Charles Hampden-Turner), *Seven Cultures of Capitalism*, Doubleday, New York, 1993.

——, *Riding the Waves of Culture, Understanding Cultural Diversity in Business*, McGraw-Hill, New York, 1997.

——, *Building Cross-Cultural Competence*, John Wiley & Sons, New York 2000.

——, *21 Leaders for the 21st Century*, Capstone Publishing Ltd, Oxford, 2001.

——, *Management dilemma's — keuze, integratie en verzoening*, Het Financieele dagblad/Business Contact, Amsterdam, 2002.

——, *Business Across Cultures*, Capstone Publishing Ltd, New York, 2003.

——(with Charles Hampden-Turner), "Response to Geert Hofstede," in *The International Journal of Intercultural Relations*, vol. 21, 1997.

Vandendriessche, Filip, *De input-output manager*, Lannoo, Tielt, 1996.

Weber, Max, *The Theory of Social and Economic Organization*, translation A. M. Henderson & Talcott Parsons, The Free Press, New York, 1947.

——, A selection of the work of Max Weber, editors I. Gadourek, G. Kuiper, J.M.G. Thurlings and A.C. Zijderveld (Eds.), *Sociologische Monografieën*, Van Logum Slaterus, Deventer, 1975.

Weick, Karl E., *The Social Psychology of Organizing*, McGraw-Hill, New York, 1979.

# About the Author

Mijnd Huijser is a cross-cultural management consultant. He worked in joint assignments with Geert Hofstede's Training Institute, Trompenaars-Hampden-Turner, and the Royal Institute of the Tropics in the Netherlands.

He holds an academic degree in philosophy and cultural anthropology. He lived and worked for more than fifteen years in Southeast Asia, the Middle East, and France.

Mijnd Huijser is the founder of CMC-Culture & Management Consulting, specializing in challenges arising from the cooperation between North American, European, Japanese, and Chinese companies. In addition to cultural awareness workshops, he focuses on cross-cultural confidence building and conflict management. Currently he works with 3M, Accenture, Clifford Chance, Canon, DSM, ING, Mitsubishi, Nissan-Renault, Philips, and Unilever.

He is the author, with Karolien Bais, of *The Profit of Peace — Corporate Responsibility in Conflict Regions* (Business Contact Amsterdam, 2004, and Greenleaf Publishers UK, 2005), on culture and the ethical dilemmas of international business in failing states. To learn more about his company: www.cmc-net.org. To contact the author: info@cmc-net.org